THE TOP 100 HERBAL REMEDIES

THE TOP 100 HERBAL REMEDIES

DUNCAN BAIRD PUBLISHERS

LONDON

The Top 100 Herbal Remedies
Anne McIntyre

For Tessa

First published in the United Kingdom and Ireland in 2006 by
Duncan Baird Publishers Ltd
Sixth Floor
Castle House
75–76 Wells Street
London W1T 3QH

Conceived, created and designed by Duncan Baird Publishers

Managing Editor: Grace Cheetham
Editor: Judy Barratt
Managing Designer: Manisha Patel
Designer: Sailesh Patel
Commissioned photography: Matthew Ward
Picture research: Louise Glasson

Library of Congress Cataloging-in-Publication Data is available

Distributed in the United States by Publishers Group West

10 9 8 7 6 5 4 3 2 1

ISBN-10: 1-84483-253-8   ISBN-13: 9-781844-832538

Typeset in Helvetica Condensed
Color reproduction by Scanhouse, Malaysia
Printed in Singapore by Imago

Publisher's Note: *The Top 100 Herbal Remedies* is not intended as a replacement for professional medical treatment and advice. The publishers and author cannot accept responsibility for any damage incurred as a result of any of the therapeutic methods contained in this work. It is advisable to consult a medical practitioner before using any of the therapeutic methods mentioned in this book, particularly if you are suffering from a medical condition or if you are pregnant.

CONTENTS

KEY

Nervous system	
Skin and eyes	
Musculo-skeletal system	
Respiratory system	
Circulatory system	
Immune system	
Digestive system	
Urinary system	
Reproductive system	
First aid	

HERBS: the original medicine

Herbs have always been central to our lives. The plant world provides us with the foods we enjoy and the air we breathe. It is hardly surprising therefore that it supplies us with remedies for treating our everyday ills, too; cultures all over the world have used these remedies for thousands of years. Our kitchen cupboards, our gardens and our hedgerows are full of potent medicines for almost every common ailment.

We have much to thank our ancestors for. Their insights into the successful use of indigenous foods and plants as medicines have survived through generations to give us a rich, global heritage of herbal medicine. The earliest records of herbal medicine originate from China and date back to around 2500BCE. The Ebers Papyrus from Egypt, which dates from around 1500BCE, mentions more than 700 herbal remedies, many of which are still popular today. We know that several other peoples – notably the Greeks, Persians, Indians and Aztecs – used medicinal plants beyond 1000BCE. These plants have provided the source for our medicines ever since.

However, in the second half of the nineteenth century, the rapid development of science and chemistry saw a steep decline in the popularity of herbs. Chemists began to isolate and extract the therapeutically active substances within the herbs and soon the tradition of healing using the whole plant fell away. Before long, scientists were able to manufacture synthetic versions of these active ingredients and the herbs, which had been revered for so long, were viewed as old-fashioned and obsolete.

Nevertheless, despite the use of sophisticated drugs and our modern-day calls for scientific proof in everything, in the last 20 years we have witnessed an enormous surge in interest in herbal medicine. Indeed, traditional plant remedies continue to provide around 85 per cent of the world's medicines. They are just as valuable today as they ever were.

MODERN MEDICINE'S DEBT TO HERBS

From a "scientific" point of view, many herbal medicines are considered to be experimental and unreliable. However, humanity has been using herbal medicines safely and successfully for thousands of years. Scientists developed many of the familiar and potent medicines of the twenty-first century from herbs, the constituents of which have provided the blueprint for many of the most effective and widely known drugs in use today. For example, quinine, the anti-malaria drug, is extracted from cinchona, found in the bark of a South-American tree; vincristine, the anti-tumour drug, comes from the Madagascan periwinkle; morphine and codeine come from the beautiful opium poppy. Atropine, aspirin, digoxin and ephedrine are all plant-derived drugs of unquestionable value. Long before the discovery of modern antibiotics, echinacea – a beautiful plant of the daisy family – was one of the most commonly prescribed remedies for infections. Of course, we now know for sure that echinacea can boost the activity of our immune system and stimulate the body's production of infection-fighting white blood cells.

Since the nineteenth century, the chemical analysis of plants has laid the foundations of a more scientific approach to herbalism. As interest into herbal medicine increases, scientists are undertaking a corresponding amount of research. All over the world they are looking into the properties of more and more foods and herbs in the belief that they will provide new cures for illnesses such as heart disease and cancer. They are making exciting discoveries that support our ancient ancestors' beliefs in herbal treatments: remedies such as ginger for arthritis, onion for the heart, garlic for infections, and turmeric for gout, have been found to have scientific merit after all; to have a basis in fact, not merely in folklore.

In the first few years of their renewed popularity, herbs were hailed as miracle remedies and panaceas, and because they are "natural" they were said to be devoid of the side-effects of orthodox medicines. A rebound effect then followed: far from championing herbal remedies, one article after another began to raise concerns about their safety. With insufficient real evidence to guide them, the public and professionals alike are susceptible to media hype. However, my great hope is that as more up-to-date, accurate information becomes readily available, we will all learn that herbal remedies are immensely effective – but only if we use them correctly. Anyone using herbs needs to be aware of their possible risks as well as their benefits.

Nevertheless the empirical evidence gathered over thousands of years, and proven by recent research, means that those who want to use herbs may rest assured that the medicine of the herbalist is based on strong foundations. Today's herbalists have the best of both worlds: their practice is based on a thorough knowledge of the traditional uses of plant medicines, as well as constantly updated scientific research.

USING THE WHOLE PLANT

Until recently the world of science has regarded plants merely as a source of active ingredients, made up of chemicals that can be separated out, analyzed and assessed in terms of biochemistry. As scientists put plants under the microscope and identified their active ingredients, they isolated single constituents, which they then used to replace whole-plant medicines. The belief of pharmacologists was that if a man-made product was similar to one derived from the plant world, the body would assimilate it in a similar way. In addition they believed that the man-made version was, in fact, superior to the natural constituent of a plant, because it was not subject to the relatively random laws of nature. Essentially, because its active ingredients were more easily measured, the man-made dosage was more reliable. Herbalists, on the other hand, prefer to treat their patients using the whole plant, believing this to be a gentler and safer form of treatment. They believe that, by isolating and synthesizing potent active ingredients, man-made remedies are likely to increase the risk of toxicity in the body and create unwanted side-effects. Another herbalist's maxim is "the whole plant is greater than the sum of its constituent parts".

There are two different types of substance found in medicinal plants, and each has an important role to play in the healing process. The primary healing agents are the active ingredients that the early chemists were interested in extracting. Most healing plants contain several active substances, one of which will be dominant. It is this dominant ingredient that influences the choice of plant by the herbal practitioner when making up a prescription for a patient. The secondary healing agents are substances such as hormones, enzymes and trace elements. We should never underestimate the importance of the secondary healing agents, because without them the active substances could have totally different effects on the body. Secondary agents act as catalysts, enhancing the action of the plants by ensuring that the body adequately absorbs and assimilates all the active constituents – dominant or otherwise. At the same time the secondary agents buffer the active constituents' more powerful actions in a variety of ways to prevent side-effects. It is the natural combination of both types of substance that determines the healing power and safety of the herbal medicines we use.

There is no better way to illustrate this than by examples – and the world of herbs is full of them. Take meadowsweet: this plant, with pretty white flowers, contains salicylic acid, which is the plant's active constituent and has an action that is similar to aspirin. It is widely known that aspirin itself can cause internal bleeding in people with sensitive stomach linings. However, herbalists actually use meadowsweet to treat an inflamed or bleeding stomach lining. The plant's secondary agents include tannin and mucilage, both of which act to protect and heal the mucous membrane of the stomach. So, while aspirin's side-effects go unchecked; meadowsweet has its own internal balancer. To illustrate this point further, most diuretic drugs (which promote urination) cause the body to lose potassium. As a result when doctors prescribe diuretics, they also need to prescribe a potassium supplement to rectify the imbalance. Herbalists use dandelion leaves as a diuretic. These leaves are themselves rich in potassium, thus combining a non-toxic diuretic with an integral potassium supplement. Finally, ephedra (*Ephedra sinica*) is a plant that the Chinese have used for thousands of years for its medicinal benefits. In relatively modern times chemists have extracted the alkaloid ephedrine from the plant, which doctors today prescribe as a treatment for myriad conditions, including nasal congestion, bronchial coughs, and asthma. Some reports claim that on its own ephedrine raises blood pressure. In the whole ephedra plant there are six other alkaloids, and the predominant one actually prevents any increase in blood pressure or in heart rate. Time and again we can see that the isolated active constituents can have serious side-effects on our well-being; while the whole plant keeps itself, and us, in balance.

WHAT IS A HERB?

By definition a herb is any plant that has a therapeutic action in the body. Naturally, this includes most of the fruit and vegetable kingdom, and not only the flowers or berries – leaves, barks, stems and roots can be medicinal too.

Herbs are very much like foods, and in fact the dividing line between them is extremely thin. For example, raspberries are full of vitamins and minerals, but in addition to their nutritional value and their delicious taste, they have been used for thousands of years to treat throat and chest problems. Furthermore, the whole raspberry plant is well known for a variety of applications during pregnancy and childbirth. Garlic and onions are excellent health-promoting and medicinal foods. They benefit the heart and circulation, contain immune-boosting sulphur and germanium and the antioxidant selenium, and so are well known for their ability to enhance the immune system, reduce levels of cholesterol, and as antioxidants to prevent damage by free radicals and degenerative disease and cancer. Celery seeds and celery itself have cleansing and antiseptic effects throughout the urinary tract, and are widely used for arthritis; oats are a wonderful tonic for the nervous system.

The vitamins, minerals and trace elements contained in herbs provide our bodies with the raw materials for recovery. Meanwhile, the herbs' other medicinal agents – such as volatile oils, bitters, tannins and alkaloids – act more specifically, each having an affinity for a particular system or organ within the body.

WHAT CAN HERBS DO?

All medicinal plants contain a range of different therapeutic agents and therefore have a variety of different actions. For example, in sage the essential oil in the leaves lends the herb its characteristic odour, and provides antiseptic and fungicidal properties. Sage leaves also contain tannin, which is astringent (it contracts the body's tissues), and a bitter compound called picrosalvine, which aids digestion. The combined effect of these components gives sage tea its disinfectant action, making it wonderful to use in gargles for sore throats and mouthwashes for inflamed gums. When we swallow the tea, other qualities of the plant come into their own – including the ability to protect us against night sweats. When breast-feeding mothers begin to wean their babies, constituents in sage tea can help to abate the flow of milk. The volatile oil in sage contains a substance called thujone.

This means that if a woman drinks sage tea on a regular basis over a long period of time or in large amounts, the tea can bring on menstrual flow. For this reason pregnant women should never drink sage tea; while expectant mothers waiting for the arrival of an overdue baby can use it to stimulate contractions.

The way in which we use a herb can also have a dramatic influence on its effects on the body. Linseeds (or flax seeds) provide a good example. We can grind the seeds into a fine powder to use as a poultice to heal skin infections. Steep the seeds in water and, because they contain a lot of mucilage, they will swell and form a thick paste. When the water is hot, the paste itself is hot. Apply this externally and it acts as a remedy for chills and pains. If you soak the seeds in cold water and take them regularly in the morning or evening, they act as an excellent mechanical laxative. Or you can take them for their tranquillizing effects. Finally, we can use linseed oil in creams to soothe eczema and cradle cap.

THE TOP TEN ACTIONS OF HERBS

1. Herbs relax overtense tissues and organs, especially the muscles and the nervous system.
2. Herbs stimulate "atonic" tissues and organs, such as a sluggish bowel or liver.
3. Herbs astringe; that is, they cause over-relaxed tissues, such as muscles, blood vessels and mucous membranes, to constrict.
4. Herbs sedate overactive areas, such as the bowel or nervous system.
5. Herbs detoxify; that is, they promote the elimination of wastes and poisons from the liver, bowel, kidneys, lungs and skin.
6. Herbs help to overcome infection through their own antiseptic, antibiotic and antifungal actions, as well as by stimulating the body's defences.
7. Herbs enhance the circulation of blood and lymph through the body.
8. Herbs aid appetite and digestion and stimulate our absorption and assimilation of nutrients, as well as providing many nutrients themselves.
9. Herbs soothe mucous membranes and thereby reduce irritation and inflammation.
10. Herbs regulate hormone production, and the action of the hormones on the body.

THE HERBAL PHARMACY

There are many ways for us to take herbs so that we can benefit from their therapeutic effects. As long as the herbs interact with the body's chemistry in one way or another, they will exert their influence. The most obvious way for us to take herbs is in our diet. Salads with basil, coriander leaves, rocket and parsley; vinaigrette with garlic; fish with dill or sorrel; new potatoes with fresh mint; biscuits and curries with ginger;

and pizza with oregano are often unknowingly our daily medicine.

As we absorb these foods in our digestive tract, the therapeutic constituents of the herbs enter the bloodstream and then circulate around the body. Most of the common culinary herbs contain a high proportion of volatile oils with antimicrobial (infection-fighting) properties. Before the days of refrigeration, these would have been vital for health (to kill off any bacteria on the food), as well as showing off a chef's culinary skills.

The skin provides a large, highly absorbent surface area. One simple way to administer herbs is to apply them to the skin where tiny capillaries under the surface will take the herbal constituents into the bloodstream. Massage in diluted essential oils, and rub in tincture-based lotions, ointments and creams, as well as compresses and poultices. In addition, we can use fresh herbs such as dock leaves to soothe a nettle sting, and yarrow leaves, or marigold or lavender flowers, to staunch bleeding from minor cuts and abrasions and to relieve a minor burn.

The delicate mucous membranes covering each eyeball (the conjunctiva) are also good at absorbing herbal extracts. An eyebright or a chamomile eye bath or a marigold compress will relieve sore and inflamed eyes. The nose and the nerve endings lying in it can provide another therapeutic pathway – one that aromatherapists use as the basis for their work. By inhalation the messages from the herbs are carried to the brain and also to the lungs where they are absorbed with oxygen into the bloodstream, and then circulated throughout the body.

Human bodies are supremely well-adapted to metabolize plant constituents as they occur in nature, meaning that when we use herbs there is little risk of side-effects or aggravations. However, it is important that we use all plant remedies in as natural a state as possible, including making sure that they are organic and free from chemical sprays and other human pollutants.

When you pick herbs make sure that you gather them away from roadsides and from cultivated land that farmers may have sprayed with pesticides or chemical fertilizers. Also be careful not to over-pick the same area or gather from places where the plant is scarce (several valued herbs are becoming increasingly rare, and even under threat of extinction), and avoid any plant that looks stunted or diseased. When you buy herbs from a store, try to check that they have come from a sustainable source.

USING HERBS

TAKING HERBS INTERNALLY

All you have to do with many herbal remedies is eat them. Remedies such as garlic, oats, cinnamon and ginger are common cooking ingredients, so include these and some of the more unusual remedies in your meals. Try adding dandelion leaves to sandwiches, or marigold flowers to an otherwise ordinary salad. There are also many other ways of enjoying the therapeutic benefits of herbs from the inside. The following are the internal preparations I have suggested in this book. Dosages are given in the table on pp.18–19.

Teas

A herbal tea is made in one of two ways – as an infusion or a decoction.

Infusions are made using the parts of the herb that grow above ground (the aerial parts), including the leaves and flowers. You can use dried or fresh herbs, but if you are using dried herbs use a ratio of 1 tsp per cup of water; for fresh herbs use 2 tsp per cup. Work on a ratio of 28g (1oz) herb per 600ml (1 pint) water. Infuse the herbs for around ten minutes in boiling water and then strain the tea into your cup. Or, if your infusion is for a child, use half or quarter measures. Make your infusions in a teapot as the lid prevents the volatile oils – with their beneficial effects – escaping into the air.

There are some herbs that are best infused using cold water, particularly those with a high mucilage content, such as marsh mallow. Place the herbs in a cold teapot and allow them to steep in cold water for between ten and 12 hours.

Most infusions are best taken hot, although if you have a urinary tract infection take the infusion lukewarm or even cold, so that the constituents of the plant are excreted by the kidneys rather than the skin. You can strain any leftover infusion into an airtight container and store it in the refrigerator for up to 48 hours.

Decoctions are made using the woody parts of the plant, such as the roots and bark. You can crush or chop the plant into small pieces. The ratio of herb to water is exactly the same as for infusions, although because decoctions are made by simmering the herb in boiling water it is good idea to add a little extra liquid to allow for evaporation. Place the chopped herb in a saucepan and pour in the cold water. Place the pan on the heat and once the water is boiling, cover it with a lid and leave it to simmer for ten to 15 minutes. Strain the decoction into your cup or, if you are storing it, into an airtight container.

Tinctures

Although they require more preparation time, tinctures are easier to store than teas, and will last almost indefinitely (although it is best to take them within two years). They are made by steeping the plant in a mixture of alcohol and water. The ratio of alcohol to water depends upon which constituent you want to extract from the herb, but the range tends to be one part herb to between two and ten parts liquid; and in that liquid you might use only 25 per cent alcohol to extract tannins, but up to 90 per cent to extract resins or gums. In practice you can make most tinctures using brandy or vodka, as the alcohol content in these spirits is about 45 per cent – which is adequate to extract the constituents of most common herbs, such as chamomile. (If you are making tinctures to give to children, or others who should avoid alcohol, you can substitute glycerol – a sugar solution – or cider vinegar for the alcohol. Make a mixture comprising 80 to 100 per cent glycerol or cider vinegar.)

Finely chop or crush fresh or dried herbs and then place the herbs in a large glass jar. For most dried herbs a ratio of one part herb to five parts

alcohol mixture works well; for fresh herbs use one part herb to two parts alcohol mixture. Seal the jar with an airtight lid and leave the herbs to macerate in the liquid for at least 14 days. Keep the jar away from direct sunlight and give it a good shake every day. Once you are ready to bottle your tincture, you will need to press out as much of the liquid as possible. A wine press is ideal for this process, although you could also sieve and squeeze the liquid through a muslin bag. Store the strained tincture in a dark-glass bottle, and keep it in a cool place.

As well as taking tinctures mixed with a little water or juice (see pp.18–19), you can also add a few drops to bath water, or mix a tincture with water for compresses, mouthwashes or gargles, or with aqueous cream for topical treatments.

Throat sprays, gargles and mouthwashes

To make a throat spray, gargle or mouthwash, dilute 1 tsp tincture in ½ cup water, or use ½ cup cooled herbal tea (whichever tea is appropriate for your ailment). You can also make a throat spray using 5 drops essential oil in ½ cup water. For the spray buy an atomizer from your chemist and aim for the back of your throat. For a gargle or mouthwash, take a mouthful of the liquid, gargle with it or swill it around your mouth, and spit it out. Repeat until the mixture has gone.

Tablets, capsules and powders

Some herbs, especially bitter herbs (such as dandelion) are best taken as teas or tinctures, because their action on the taste buds triggers part of their therapeutic effects by stimulating digestion. However, one of the most convenient ways to take many herbs is in the form of capsules or tablets. Standard preparations should be fairly easy to find in your local herbal store. However, if you want to make your own specific combinations, buy some empty capsules and the powdered form of the relevant herbs. Scoop the combined powders into the capsules, or use a capsule-maker. You can also use herbal powder topically to treat many skin complaints.

Medicinal honeys

A teaspoon of medicinal honey is one of the best ways for children to take herbs. Finely chop the herb (either fresh or dried), or crush it finely, and cover it with honey. Allow the herb to steep in the honey for as long as possible (up to two years). Alternatively, place 1 drop essential oil into 1 tsp honey and administer the medicine this way.

Steam inhalations

To make a steam inhalation fill a bowl with hot water enriched with 5 to 10 drops essential oil; or fill the bowl with a standard infusion or decoction. Place a towel over your head, lean over the bowl and breathe deeply for between five and ten minutes.

TAKING HERBS EXTERNALLY

The skin is able to absorb most of the therapeutic properties of herbs. The following are known as external preparations because they work their magic from the outside in. Dosages are given in the table on pp.18–19.

Herbal baths

Immersing yourself in a relaxing herbal bath allows the properties of the herbs to enter the body through the skin's pores, which open up in the warm water. The herbs also enter through the mouth and nose, as you breathe in the steam from the bath. Overall, the route to your blood and nervous system is fast as it bypasses the lengthy process of digestion.

Herbal baths are particularly useful to relax and soothe the nervous system and to ease mental and emotional strain. Some of the best herbs to use in this way are lavender, basil, rose and chamomile, which are not only fragrant but also soothing. Chamomile is particularly good for fractious children, especially when they are unwell, for not only does it possess antimicrobial properties, but it also helps to induce sleep – nature's best way to ward off infection and enable self-healing. Rosemary baths, while relaxing, have a stimulating edge as they enhance blood-flow to the head and enable greater alertness and concentration.

Hand and foot baths

Traditionally, mustard foot baths were used for all the afflictions rife in cold and damp climates – from colds and flu to poor circulation and arthritis. Maurice Messegue, a famous French herbalist, popularized hand and foot baths in the mid-twentieth century, and wrote several books on herbal therapy based only on these forms of treatment. The hands and feet are rich in nerve endings and so, according to Messegue, despite some thickening of the skin as a result of use, are highly sensitive areas of the skin, where the herbal constituents pass easily from the skin into the body. Hand and foot baths are excellent ways to treat babies and children, who love to splash in the water.

Eye baths

Eye baths enable the eyes to benefit from the therapeutic properties of herbs for all manner of eye complaints, from tired eyes to styes, as the conjunctiva – the membranes covering the eyes – absorb the active properties of the herbs. Always use a clean eye bath (available from pharmacies) and fresh solution for each eye.

Ointments, creams and lotions

It is not only skin problems that benefit from the application of ointments, creams and lotions. Headaches and inflamed joints – among other things – can benefit, too.

To make an ointment place as much fresh or dried herb as possible into a heatproof bowl. Add 450ml (¾ pint) olive oil and 50g (2oz) beeswax. Place the bowl over a pan of boiling water on a low heat. Leave the herbs to macerate like this for two to four hours. Then press the contents through a muslin bag, to squeeze out the liquid. Pour this into ointment jars and leave to solidify.

To make a cream you will need a neutral base, such as aqueous cream (available from pharmacies). For every 50g (2oz) base cream stir in 2 or 3 drops essential oil, or 5 to 10 ml tincture or double-strength decoction.

Lotions are excellent topical remedies for skin conditions and minor injuries. To make a lotion mix 50 per cent water with 50 per cent dilute tincture, or use a double-strength infusion or decoction, or 2 or 3 drops oil, per 10ml water.

Compresses

A herbal compress is a wonderful way to relieve headaches, stomach pain, backache and joint pain, as well as to help to clear spots and boils. Soak a clean piece of cotton (such as a clean flannel) in a hot or cold tea, or 1 tsp tincture in 20ml water, or 10ml water laced with 2 drops essential oil diluted in 1 tsp base oil (such as sesame oil). Once the cotton is totally wet, squeeze out the excess liquid and place the compress on the affected area. Hold it there for ten minutes. Repeat as often as possible.

Poultices

A poultice is similar to a compress except that you apply the herb itself, rather than its extract, to the affected area. If you are using fresh leaves, stems or roots, bruise them to release their therapeutic properties. If you are using powdered or finely chopped dry herbs, add them to a little hot water to make a paste. Place your herbs between two pieces of gauze and then, using a light cotton bandage, bind the poultice to the skin and keep it warm using a hot water bottle.

Essential oils

Essential oils are widely available from herbal pharmacies and health stores. They are extracted from aromatic plants through a process of steam distillation and are extremely concentrated. Always follow the dilution guidelines on the bottle before any essential oil comes into contact with your skin. You can also use essential oils in burners to permeate the atmosphere or in inhalations for a variety of ailments, such as colds, catarrh, coughs, insomnia and anxiety.

FINDING THE RIGHT DOSAGE

Deciding upon which herbal remedy to take and how to take it depends upon the condition, your age and build, your constitution, and even the time of year. A herbal practitioner makes decisions about which herbs to use, the type of preparation, the dosage, when you should take the remedy, and the duration of treatment. In general, chronic (ongoing) conditions require mild herbal remedies, which you can take safely, usually three times a day, potentially for months at a time. Acute conditions (finite but intense bouts of illness) may require stronger remedies, and you may need to take them up to every two hours. Some conditions, particularly fevers, colds, catarrh and problems associated with being cold, are better treated using hot preparations. Others, such as urinary problems, are better with cool preparations. Skin problems may improve more rapidly if you take herbal teas (as opposed to tinctures); while tinctures may be preferable when you require more concentrated medicines, such as in the treatment of a virulent infection. Follow the treatments on pp.70–123 precisely, and use the standard dosage (see table, pp.18–19), unless otherwise instructed.

STANDARD DOSAGES **Before using herbs it is important to understand your symptoms and if neces-sary visit your local medical practitioner or herbalist for a clear diagnosis. If acute symptoms do not clear within a few days, and chronic symptoms do not improve within 3 to 4 weeks, call in profession-al help. This table gives the standard dosage of herbal remedies for adults and children. Use these guidelines unless instructed otherwise. Never exceed the stated dose. If you are ever in any doubt about any remedy, consult a herbal practitioner for advice.**

PREPARATION	STANDARD ADULT DOSAGE	STANDARD CHILD DOSAGE
Infusions	1 cup 3 times a day for chronic illness or every 1–2 hours for acute illness	¼–½ cup every 3–4 hours for chronic illness; every 1–2 hours for acute
Decoctions	1 cup 3 times a day for chronic illness or every hour for acute illness	¼–½ cup every 3–4 hours for chronic illness; every 1–2 hours for acute
Tinctures	1 tsp in a little juice or warm water, 3–6 times a day, depending on whether the illness is chronic or acute	In a little warm water, 3–6 times a day; Babies: 5 drops; Toddlers: 10–20 drops; Ages 3–6: ¼ tsp; Ages 6–12: ½ tsp; Over 12: as adults
Throat sprays	3 times a day for chronic illness; every 2 hours for acute illness	As adults
Gargles	2–3 times a day for chronic illness; every 2 hours for acute illness	As adults
Mouthwashes	3 times a day	As adults
Capsules	Size 0: 1 or 2 capsules, 3 times a day; Size 00: one capsule, 2 times a day	Over 6 years: one size 0 capsule, 3 times a day

PREPARATION	STANDARD ADULT DOSAGE	STANDARD CHILD DOSAGE
Medicinal honeys	1–2 tsp, 3–6 times a day	½–1 tsp, 3–6 times a day
Steam inhalations	Twice daily for 5–10 minutes at a time	Over 6 years: as adults; supervised
Herbal baths	2 or 3 drops diluted essential oil or 600ml (1 pint) double-strength infusion in bathwater; soak for 10–30 minutes	1 drop essential oil diluted in 10ml base oil, such as sesame oil; bath for 10–30 minutes
Hand baths	2 or 3 drops diluted (see below) essential oil, or 1 litre (1¾ pints) double-strength tea, or 2–3 tsp tincture in a bowl of hot water for 8 minutes every morning	As for adults, but for 4 minutes every morning
Foot baths	2 or 3 drops essential oil, or 1 litre (1¾ pints) double-strength tea, or 2–3 tsp tincture in a bowl of hot water, for 8 minutes every evening	As for adults, but for 4 minutes every evening
Eye baths	10–20ml warm decoction, 3 times a day for chronic illness or every 2 hours for acute illness	As adults
Creams, lotions, ointments	Apply to the affected area 2–3 times a day	As adults
Compresses	As often as possible, for 10 minutes at a time	As adults
Poultices	Morning and night for 2–4 hours at a time	As adults
Essential oils (for massage or in bathwater)	2 drops essential oil diluted in 1 tsp (5ml) base oil, such as sesame oil	1 drop essential oil diluted in 1 tsp (5ml) base oil

YARROW *Achillea millefolium*

A summer herb, found wild in the countryside, yarrow is renowned as a remedy for bleeding.

PARTS USED
aerial parts of the flowering plant

PROPERTIES/ACTIONS:
diaphoretic • febrifuge • peripheral vasodilator • hypotensive • anti-allergenic • vulnerary • emmenagogue • styptic • anti-inflammatory • astringent • diuretic • digestive • urinary antiseptic • decongestant • hormone-regulating • detoxifying

INDICATIONS:
fever • rheumatism • heartburn • indigestion • peptic ulcers • urinary infections • bleeding piles • gastritis • heavy periods • varicose veins • catarrh • colds • flu • high blood pressure • allergies • diarrhea • irritable bowel syndrome • gall-bladder problems • fluid retention • varicose ulcers • eczema • bruises • cuts and wounds • sprains and strains • nosebleeds

Yarrow's astringent properties have a drying effect on body fluids and help to stem blood-flow, curb diarrhea and clear catarrh. The herb is also great to stimulate the appetite, enhance digestion and absorption, and relax tension in the gut. Antiseptic and anti-inflammatory, yarrow speeds healing in gastritis and enteritis. A hot tea can overcome fevers, colds and flu, and a lukewarm or cold tea relieve cystitis. Use yarrow tea externally to bathe wounds, varicose ulcers and burns, as well as hemorrhoids, and skin conditions such as eczema.

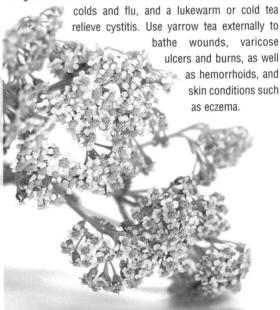

Avoid taking yarrow during pregnancy.

GARLIC *Allium sativum*

Nature's best antibiotic is also an invigorating tonic – a veritable "elixir of life".

Garlic is a powerful antimicrobial (infection-fighter). Effective throughout the digestive, respiratory and urinary systems, it is an ideal remedy for coughs, colds and flu, stomach and bowel infections, and cystitis. Garlic stimulates the secretion of digestive enzymes, and the aids the body's absorption of nutrients. It enhances the pancreas's production of insulin, making it useful for diabetics. It lowers blood pressure and cholesterol, and it has antioxidant and anti tumour activities, which help to rejuvenate the body and protect against cancer.

PARTS USED:
bulbs

PROPERTIES/ACTIONS:
general stimulant • carminative • expectorant • alterative • immune-boosting • antimicrobial • anthelmintic • probiotic • cholesterol-lowering • hypotensive • antitumour • rejuvenative • circulatory stimulant • digestive • anti-inflammatory • reproductive stimulant

INDICATIONS:
colds • flu • chest infections • GI tract infections • urinary infections • worms • high cholesterol • lowered immunity • thrush • catarrh • sinusitis • high blood pressure • atherosclerosis • earache • sore throat • laryngitis • asthma • diverticulitis • flatulence • scabies • low sperm count • splinters • toothache

Therapeutic doses of garlic should be discontinued 7 to 10 days before any surgery.

✢ ◉ ◐ ♕ ◗ ♡ ✿

ALOE VERA *Aloe vera*

PARTS USED:
dried juice of leaves

PROPERTIES/ACTIONS:
alterative • anthelmintic • digestive • laxative • bitter tonic • rejuvenative • diuretic • detoxifying • anti-inflammatory

INDICATIONS:
arthritis • fever • constipation • hot flushes • eye problems • hemorrhoids • coughs • chronic ulcers • peptic ulcers • varicose ulcers • mouth ulcers • dysentery • worms • sunburn • amenorrhea • burns and scalds• heartburn • eczema • urticaria • ringworm • psoriasis • sprains and strains

Aloe is a succulent plant with remarkable healing powers that help to keep you young.

Aloe vera juice is a gentle laxative, helping to clear toxins and microorganisms from the bowel. The juice also protects the lining of the gut, acts as a bitter tonic to the liver, aids digestion, and regulates the body's metabolism. Applied externally, aloe vera lotion will rejuvenate the skin and reduce wrinkles, while the gel relieves pain, soothes inflammation, and is mildly antibiotic. It will soothe cuts, abrasions, hemorrhoids and skin conditions such as eczema. Use the gel to treat burns, and after radiation therapy.

Do not use aloe vera if you are pregnant or experiencing any uterine bleeding.

MARSH MALLOW *Althea officinalis*

Soothing marsh mallow is wonderful for all kinds of irritation and inflammation.

Marsh mallow contains an abundance of mucilage, which coats and protects the lining of the respiratory, digestive and urinary tracts. Its expectorant properties mean that marsh mallow can soothe dry coughs, sore throats, and bronchitis. The plant will also relieve inflammatory digestive problems, such as heartburn and gastritis, and urinary problems, such as cystitis. Rub the leaves on the affected area to soothe insect bites, scalds, sunburn and rashes. A warm poultice will draw out splinters; a mouthwash will soothe sore gums.

PARTS USED:
roots • leaves • flowers

PROPERTIES/ACTIONS:
emollient • demulcent • vulnerary • anti-inflammatory • mild expectorant • diuretic • immune-boosting • painkilling

INDICATIONS:
irritation of the bronchial, GI and urinary tracts • croup • bronchitis • asthma • sore throats • heartburn • colitis • gastritis • urinary infections • skin problems, including boils • diarrhea • irritable bowel syndrome • diverticulitis • kidney stones • tired eyes • styes • burns and scalds • splinters • bites and stings

BURDOCK *Arctium lappa*

PARTS USED:
roots • leaves • seeds

PROPERTIES/ACTIONS:
bitter tonic • digestive •
diuretic • diaphoretic • laxative •
antimicrobial • alterative •
hypoglycemic •
anti-inflammatory • detoxifying

INDICATIONS:
eczema • acne • psoriasis • boils •
abscesses • measles • arthritis •
rheumatism • gout • fever •
tonsillitis • colds • flu •
candidiasis • PMS • heartburn •
acidity • flatulence • constipation •
urinary infections • fluid
retention • impetigo • cold sores •
ringworm • herpes • poor
appetite • anemia • urticaria •
warts and veruccae • styes

This handsome plant draws toxins out of the
body, making it a wonderful cleanser.

Burdock has the ability to absorb toxins from the gut and
carry them through to the bowel for elimination; its diuretic
properties clear toxins via the kidneys. A great liver remedy,
the plant can relieve inflammatory conditions such as arthritis and gout, and inflammatory skin problems such as
eczema and psoriasis. As an effective antibacterial and antifungal herb, burdock will fight all manner of infection. Apply
the poultice externally to ulcers, bruises, sores and boils; and
the decoction to impetigo, cold sores and ringworm.

WILD OATS *Avena sativa*

Nutrient-rich wild oats will boost your energy and help combat the effects of stress.

Rich in protein, calcium, magnesium, silica and iron, and a host of vitamins, oats help to make bones and teeth strong. Both strengthening and relaxing, oats can help to relieve depression, anxiety, tension, insomnia and nervous exhaustion. They also lower blood cholesterol and sugar, helping to prevent heart problems and diabetes. High in fibre, oats are great for combating constipation, and by removing toxins from the bowel are said to help prevent bowel cancer. Use oatmeal externally to soothe inflamed skin conditions.

PARTS USED:
grains

PROPERTIES/ACTIONS:
nervine • nourishing tonic • antidepressant • hypoglycemic • demulcent • vulnerary • hormone-regulating • cholesterol-lowering

INDICATIONS:
depression • nervous exhaustion • anxiety • insomnia • convalescence • cardiovascular disease • constipation • irritable bowel syndrome • diverticulitis • inflammatory skin problems • high cholesterol • neuralgia • shingles • cramp • osteoporosis • low libido • low sperm count

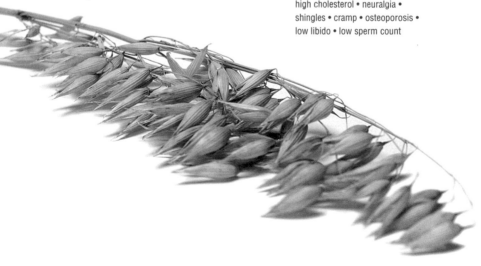

MARIGOLD *Calendula officinalis*

PARTS USED:
flowers

PROPERTIES/ACTIONS:
relaxant • alterative • astringent • antiseptic • antimicrobial • antispasmodic • anti-ulcer • anti-inflammatory • antitumour • antioxidant • antihistamine • diaphoretic • diuretic • bitter tonic • digestive • cholagogue • detoxifying • estrogenic • vulnerary

INDICATIONS:
inflammatory skin problems • digestive problems • peptic ulcers • fever • infections • minor burns and scalds • cuts and wounds • grazes • swollen glands • diarrhea • period pain • heavy periods • tender, swollen breasts • fibroids • endometriosis • menopause • varicose veins • varicose ulcers • tonsillitis • warts and veruccae • chilblains • osteoporosis • herpes • acne • urticaria • impetigo • psoriasis • tired eyes • styes • bleeding gums • splinters • toothache • sprains and strains • nosebleeds

This cheerful, golden flower takes pride of place as an antiseptic, first-aid remedy.

Marigold enhances immunity and helps the body fight bacterial, fungal and viral infections. In the digestive tract it relieves irritation and inflammation and aids digestion and nutrient-absorption. Taken as a hot tea, marigold brings down fevers, improves blood and lymphatic circulation, and regulates menstruation. In the uterus it clears the congestion that contributes to period pain, excessive bleeding, fibroids and cysts. Apply marigold externally to soothe cuts, sores, skin problems, varicose veins, warts, burns, and cold sores.

Avoid taking marigold in any form during pregnancy.

GOTU COLA *Centella asiatica, Hydrocotyle asiatica*

A wonderful brain tonic, gotu cola boosts our brain power and keeps us young.

Gotu cola aids memory and concentration and has proved excellent in helping children with autism and learning difficulties, including ADHD (attention deficit hyperactivity disorder). It relieves stress, anxiety, insomnia and depression, and soothes indigestion, acidity and diarrhea, and helps to clear skin problems. By stimulating healing in the connective tissue, gotu cola helps wounds knit together and reduces scarring. Apply the oil to your head and feet at night to prevent insomnia, or rub it into your scalp to prevent early balding and greying in your hair.

PARTS USED:
leaves

PROPERTIES/ACTIONS:
nervine • cardiac tonic • immune-boosting • febrifuge • alterative • diuretic • antiseptic • anthelmintic • vulnerary • rejuvenative • hair tonic • anticonvulsant • anxiolytic • analgesic • anti-inflammatory • painkilling • circulatory stimulant

INDICATIONS:
skin problems • cuts and wounds • anxiety • depression • convalescence • poor memory and concentration • learning problems • childhood infections • urinary infections • insomnia • fever • Alzheimer's disease • headaches • exhaustion • worms

BLACK COHOSH *Cimicifuga racemosa*

PARTS USED:
roots • rhizomes

PROPERTIES/ACTIONS:
sedative • antispasmodic • anti-inflammatory • antirheumatic • hypotensive • emmenagogue • estrogenic • uterine tonic • painkilling • astringent

INDICATIONS:
headaches • nerve and muscle pain • breast pain • mastitis • cramp • colic • asthma • whooping cough • tinnitus • high blood pressure • palpitations • arthritis • menopause • PMS • period pain • heavy periods • endometriosis • nervous tension • earache • arthritis • rheumatism • osteoporosis • bursitis and tendonitis

Native Americans once used black cohosh to ease childbirth, giving it the name "squaw root".

Black cohosh is a powerful painkiller (it contains salicylates, used to make aspirin), relieving all kinds of pain including muscle and nerve pain, cramp, arthritis pain, uterine and breast pain, and headaches. The herb dilates the arteries and so can help to reduce high blood pressure and normalize the action of the heart. Its estrogenic properties can be helpful in relieving the symptoms of the menopause, and in curbing PMS and painful periods. During childbirth, black cohosh can stimulate contractions in the uterus.

CINNAMON *Cinnamomum zeylanicum*

Warming and strengthening, cinnamon eases colds and congestion and restores energy.

Delicious-tasting cinnamon stimulates the circulation and causes sweating, which helps us to overcome flu, colds and fevers. Myriad chronic and acute infections are warded off by cinnamon's powerful antibacterial, antifungal and antiviral properties, including cystitis and tonsillitis, as well as persistent conditions such as ME. Cinnamon will help to dry up nosebleeds and catarrh, and lighten heavy periods. Apply it locally to ease the pain of arthritis and tooth- or headache. Use it as an antiseptic wash for wounds, stings and head lice.

PARTS USED:
inner bark

PROPERTIES/ACTIONS:
astringent • hemostatic • antispasmodic • stomachic • carminative • antiseptic • invigorating • immune-boosting • diaphoretic • restorative • antimicrobial • circulatory stimulant

INDICATIONS:
colds • sinusitis • coughs • fever • flu • nosebleeds • stress • ME/post-viral syndrome • arthritis • rheumatism • toothache • headaches • muscle stiffness • candidiasis • colic • flatulence • diarrhea • nausea • cuts and wounds • bites and stings • infective skin complaints • head lice • tonsillitis • bronchitis • ringworm • low libido

Avoid taking cinnamon during pregnancy.

CORIANDER *Coriandrum sativum*

PARTS USED:
ripe seeds • leaves

PROPERTIES/ACTIONS:
carminative • diuretic • decongestant • antispasmodic • antimicrobial • diaphoretic • digestive • circulatory stimulant • refrigerant • anti-inflammatory • detoxifying

INDICATIONS:
flu • colds • coughs • urinary infections • flatulence • skin problems • allergies • measles • gastritis • fever • conjunctivitis • sore throats • peptic ulcers • arthritis • colic • abdominal pain • period pain • anemia • acne • urticaria

Once considered an aphrodisiac, coriander is best known as an excellent aid to digestion.

Coriander enhances the appetite and improves the body's absorption of nutrients. The leaves themselves are rich in vitamins A and C, as well as calcium, potassium and iron. The herb has long been known as a tonic for the brain and nerves, and its cooling effects will calm fevers and inflammatory problems, such as cystitis, sore throats, hay fever and arthritis, and reduce hot flushes. Apply the leaves' juice or the tea externally to relieve hot, itchy skin rashes. The tea also makes a great gargle for sore throats and oral thrush.

HAWTHORN *Crataegus monogyna*

A "food for the heart", hawthorn is the best herb to strengthen the heart and balance circulation.

If you suffer from atherosclerosis (thickened arterial walls), try hawthorn, which softens deposits in the arteries. Hawthorn is excellent for high blood pressure, low blood pressure and angina, and to regulate the heart, helping to overcome arrhythmias and palpitations. The berries are astringent and will help to cure diarrhea. Make a tea using the leaves, flowers and berries together to treat indigestion; apply a decoction of the flowers and berries to acne, or use it as a gargle to relieve a sore throat.

PARTS USED:
berries • leaves • flowers

PROPERTIES/ACTIONS:
cardiac tonic • hypotensive • vasodilator • astringent • relaxant • antispasmodic • diuretic • emollient • vulnerary • anti-inflammatory • mild expectorant • circulatory stimulant • digestive

INDICATIONS:
high/low blood pressure • anemia • atherosclerosis • indigestion • heart disease • palpitations • arrhythmia • breathlessness • diarrhea • anxiety • angina • acne • sore throats • arthritis • muscle pain • high cholesterol • bleeding gums

WILD YAM *Dioscorea villosa*

PARTS USED:
roots • rhizomes

PROPERTIES/ACTIONS:
antispasmodic • antirheumatic • diuretic • anti-inflammatory • cholagogue • relaxant • peripheral vasodilator • expectorant • estrogenic • emmenagogue • hormone-regulating

INDICATIONS:
amenorrhea • prolapse • endometriosis • fibroids • irregular periods • menstrual cramps • birth contractions • post-partum hemorrhage • pain after childbirth • tension • nausea • anxiety • infertility • PMS • period pain • osteoporosis • muscular spasm • rheumatoid arthritis • bowel inflammation • colic • urinary infections • diverticulitis • flatulence • breast benign disorder • irritable bowel syndrome • flatulence • gall-bladder problems • muscle pain • low libido

Wild yam's roots contain substances similar to progesterone, making this the "woman's herb".

Whether you suffer from PMS or menstrual problems, or are going through the menopause, wild yam is one of the best herbs to correct hormonal imbalances. The plant provides a substance called diosgenin, which pharmacists once used in the manufacture of the contraceptive pill to mimic the hormone progesterone and prevent ovulation. Wild yam's antispasmodic properties ease menstrual cramping, muscular spasm, colic, and flatulence. Its anti-inflammatory properties make wild yam a good remedy for arthritis and gout.

ECHINACEA *Echinacea angustifolia*

Echinacea is renowned for its antibiotic action and its ability to boost immunity.

Echinacea helps the immune system to produce infection-fighting white cells in our blood. It can prevent and treat a host of bacterial, viral and fungal infections, including tonsillitis, colds, flu, sinusitis, and glandular fever. By stimulating circulation, echinacea can promote sweating, helping us to overcome fever; as an anti-inflammatory it can treat arthritis, gout, and pelvic inflammatory disease. The tincture makes a good mouthwash for gum disease and a wash for wounds, sores and stings.

PARTS USED:
roots • rhizomes

PROPERTIES/ACTIONS:
immune-boosting • antiseptic • antimicrobial • diaphoretic • anti-allergenic • lymphatic tonic • antibiotic • peripheral vasodilator • vulnerary • anti-inflammatory

INDICATIONS:
septicemia • catarrh • pyorrhea • tonsillitis • boils • laryngitis • candidiasis • sinusitis • eczema • urticaria • gingivitis • allergies • ME/post-viral syndrome • glandular fever • arthritis • gout • tiredness • colds • flu • earache • bursitis and tendonitis • herpes • acne • impetigo • scabies • toothache

BONESET *Eupatorium perfoliatum*

PARTS USED:
aerial parts of the flowering plant

PROPERTIES/ACTIONS:
diaphoretic • febrifuge • aperient •
general tonic • antispasmodic •
peripheral vasodilator • alterative •
cholagogue • mild laxative •
expectorant • decongestant

INDICATIONS:
flu • colds • acute bronchitis •
catarrh • muscular rheumatism •
poor circulation • constipation •
skin problems • night sweats •
fever • osteoporosis

A member of the hemp family, boneset is the perfect antidote to the first signs of flu.

Boneset encourages circulation to your muscles to relieve the aches and pains that herald the onset of flu, helps throw off fevers, and clears congestion. Rheumatism and similar muscular pains also respond well to boneset. Its laxative effects can help to ease constipation. Boneset can also treat skin conditions linked with poor liver function. Recent research indicates that the herb may help fight cancer as it contains lactones that may prevent secondary tumours, and flavones, which encourage the healthy functioning of cells.

EYEBRIGHT *Euphrasia officinalis*

With its pretty white flowers that look like eyes, eyebright is the best remedy for eye problems.

An eyebright decoction is wonderful as a tea, but also makes an eyewash or a soak for a compress to treat myriad eye irritations. Whether you suffer from light-sensitivity, a stye, conjunctivitis, or blepharitis, eyebright will help to reduce inflammation and soothe sore eyes. Its anti-inflammatory and decongestant properties make it great for treating upper respiratory tract conditions, for relieving nasal congestion, sinusitis, hay fever, and colds. As a bitter tonic, eyebright aids digestion and assists liver function.

PARTS USED:
leaves • flowers
PROPERTIES/ACTIONS:
astringent • anti-inflammatory • general tonic • decongestant • digestive • cholagogue • alterative
INDICATIONS:
hay fever • nasal catarrh • sinusitis • conjunctivitis and other eye infections • tired eyes • light-sensitivity • gum disease • sore throats • indigestion • heartburn

MEADOWSWEET *Filipendula ulmaria*

PARTS USED:
aerial parts of the flowering plant

PROPERTIES/ACTIONS:
astringent • antacid • stomachic • anti-emetic • antirheumatic • anti-inflammatory • antiseptic • diuretic • diaphoretic • painkilling

INDICATIONS:
arthritis • rheumatism • gout • heartburn • acidity • nausea • indigestion • gastritis • peptic ulcers • diarrhea • fever • urinary infections • kidney stones • atherosclerosis • headaches • fluid retention • bursitis and tendonitis • sciatica • tired eyes

Queen of the meadow, this herb is the natural equivalent of aspirin – without the side-effects.

Meadowsweet will protect and soothe the lining of the digestive tract, making it the perfect remedy for all digestive conditions, from heartburn to ulcers. Meadowseet contains salicylates, crystals of salicylic acid, that help to reduce inflammation in arthritis, rheumatism and gout, and soften deposits, such as kidney stones and any build-up in the arteries. Take it as a hot tea to reduce fevers and the aches and pains of flu; and to relieve headaches. Externally, apply a soothing cooled meadowsweet tea to inflamed skin or eyes.

FENNEL *Foeniculum vulgare*

This feathery herb, with its lovely aniseed aroma, will settle your digestion with ease.

For centuries people wanting to lose weight and stay young ate fennel seeds. However, fennel seeds are most effective as a digestive – settling the stomach, relieving colic and wind, and easing indigestion and heartburn. You can also boost your appetite by chewing some seeds before a meal. Fennel is also antispasmodic (use it for period pain) and diuretic (releasing excess fluid from the body). Apply the cooled tea to your skin to help to reduce wrinkles. If you are breast-feeding, fennel will help to increase milk production.

Do not take fennel if you suffer from epilepsy or during early pregnancy. Check before giving fennel to children.

PARTS USED:
seeds

PROPERTIES/ACTIONS:
digestive • antispasmodic • carminative • galactagogue • antibacterial • diuretic • general stimulant • expectorant • rubefacient • antifungal

INDICATIONS:
bronchitis • colic • flatulence • muscular and rheumatic pain • blepharitis • conjunctivitis • gout • toxic conditions • alcoholism • kidney stones • urinary infections • PMS • poor milk-flow • obesity • menopause • poor appetite • heartburn • flatulence • gastritis • gall-bladder problems • fluid retention • tired eyes • nausea

CLEAVERS *Galium aparine*

PARTS USED:
aerial parts

PROPERTIES/ACTIONS:
diuretic • alterative •
anti-inflammatory • astringent •
antitumour • general tonic •
refrigerant • mild laxative •
detoxifying

INDICATIONS:
tonsillitis • glandular fever •
enlarged adenoids • swollen
lymph glands • eczema •
psoriasis • acne • boils • fluid
retention • kidney stones •
arthritis • gout • fever •
measles • chicken pox •
urinary infections •
ulcers • earache •
sore throats •
fluid retention •
impetigo •
burns and
scalds

A common hedgerow weed, cleavers is a
wonderful cleanser and detoxifier.

Our ancestors ate cleavers' soup to lose weight, but today
cleavers is used mainly as a cleansing remedy to clear toxins
and reduce heat and inflammation. Soothing and diuretic,
cleavers is also good for cystitis, fluid retention, arthritis and
gout, and taken regularly as tea can help to clear myriad skin
conditions. If you have swollen lymph nodes (glands), cooling cleavers can help to reduce congestion and inflammation; it will also reduce fevers. Apply an infusion of cleavers
to burns and abrasions, and as a hair rinse against dandruff.

LICORICE *Glycyrrhiza glabra*

Sweet licorice will increase resilience to stress, whether physical or emotional.

If you suffer from painful inflammatory conditions such as arthritis, or allergies such as hay fever, licorice can ease discomfort, thanks largely to its glycyrrhizin, a component similar to the steroid cortisone. As an expectorant licorice is good for coughs, asthma and chest infections; and the root is well-known as a remedy for digestive problems, such as heartburn, indigestion and ulcers. Its hormone-balancing action makes it great for problems such as PMS and symptoms of the menopause.

PARTS USED:
peeled roots • runners

PROPERTIES/ACTIONS:
demulcent • expectorant • general tonic • laxative • anti-inflammatory • anti-allergenic • diaphoretic • diuretic • adaptogen • antitussive • antacid • adrenocorticotrophic • reproductive tonic • estrogenic • cholesterol-lowering • antifungal • antiviral • immune-boosting

INDICATIONS:
inflammatory problems • allergies • bronchitis • peptic ulcers • menstrual and menopausal problems • digestive problems • stress-related problems • constipation • sore throats • respiratory infections • asthma • viral infections (including herpes) • gall-bladder problems • enlarged prostate • high cholesterol • candidiasis • depression • restlessness • earache • heartburn • arthritis • hay fever • rheumatism • osteoporosis • bursitis and tendonitis • eczema • conjunctivitis • styes • irregular periods

Avoid taking licorice during pregnancy, or if you suffer from cirrhosis of the liver or high blood pressure.

⊕ ✺ ◐ ◍ ✿

HOPS *Humulus lupulus*

PARTS USED:
dried strobiles of the female plant

PROPERTIES/ACTIONS:
sedative • relaxant •
antispasmodic • bitter tonic •
digestive • astringent • diuretic •
estrogenic • painkilling • antiseptic

INDICATIONS:
stress-related digestive
problems • diarrhea • nerve
pain • insomnia • excitability •
diverticulitis • nervous indigestion •
peptic ulcers • ulcerative colitis •
Crohn's disease • irritable bowel
syndrome • colic • gut spasm •
nervous or irritable coughs •
menopause • irregular periods •
earache • osteoporosis •
muscle pain • toothache

Hops – a much-loved flavouring in beer –
will ease away tension, anxiety and pain.

Hops can calm the nervous system and are wonderful for
reducing problems related to stress. A nervous system that
is out of kilter can affect the healthy functioning of the digestive system. Hops will help to impede this link, while stimulating digestion and liver function. The stress-busting effects
reach our muscles, too: the plant's antispasmodic properties
relieve muscle tension. Regular cups of hop tea are both
diuretic and detoxifying; while the estrogenic effects of hops
make them great for relieving symptoms of the menopause.

Hops can act as
a mild depressant.
Avoid them if
you suffer from
depression.

ELECAMPANE *Inula helenium*

A stately plant with bright yellow flowers, bitter elecampane will hasten away chest infections.

Before the advent of antibiotics, doctors often treated pneumonia and tuberculosis with elecampane. Antifungal, antibacterial and expectorant, this wonderful herb will see off catarrh, colds, asthma, bronchitis, whooping cough, and other chest infections. The herb also stimulates digestion, regulates the bowels, and helps expel toxins from the body. Hot elecampane tea will bring down a fever; cooled, the tea makes a great antiseptic wash for wounds and cuts, and for skin infections such as scabies and herpes.

PARTS USED:
rhizomes

PROPERTIES/ACTIONS:
expectorant • antitussive • diaphoretic • antimicrobial • antiseptic • bitter tonic • cholagogue • anthelmintic • digestive

INDICATIONS:
bronchial coughs • bronchitis • emphysema • pneumonia • asthma • catarrh • colic • flatulence • poor digestion • rheumatism • worms • osteoporosis • herpes • scabies • cuts and wounds

LAVENDER *Lavandula officinalis*

PARTS USED:
flowers

PROPERTIES/ACTIONS:
relaxant • sedative • analgesic • antidepressant • nervine • diuretic • digestive • antispasmodic • carminative • anti-inflammatory • antimicrobial • vulnerary • antioxidant • painkilling • detoxifying • anthelmintic • refrigerant

INDICATIONS:
tension • depression • anxiety • insomnia • colds • catarrh • coughs • asthma • croup • flu • tonsillitis • laryngitis • fever • pain • headaches • migraines • muscle tension • colic • GI tract infections • burns and scalds • cuts and wounds • scars • bruises • splinters • sores • skin and mouth ulcers • inflammatory skin conditions • bites and stings • earache • worms • chilblains • bursitis and tendonitis • nerve pain • impetigo • scabies • head lice

Sweet-smelling lavender is an aromatic restorative for both mind and body.

Our grandmothers may have used lavender in their wardrobes to ward off moths, but today we are more likely to use it to relax muscles, ease anxiety, and relieve depression. Lavender is also antioxidant, protecting the body against free radicals (which speed the signs of ageing and can cause cancer), as well as decongestant, expectorant and antibacterial. Externally, gentle lavender essential oil helps minimize scarring and heal wounds, and relieves the irritation caused by insect bites and stings.

LINSEED *Linum usitatissimum*

Delicate with pretty blue flowers, soothing linseed is wonderful for rehydrating dry skin.

Make a poultice of linseed by adding boiling water to the crushed seeds and stirring the mixture into a paste. Apply the poultice to shingles, psoriasis or burns to soothe away the pain. Or, add a few drops of linseed oil to your bathwater simply to soften your skin. In a tea linseed will soothe a dry, hacking cough. It is a gentle laxative so excellent for overcoming constipation – add a few seeds to a bowl of porridge. The oil is a good source of essential fatty acids, which help support the nervous, immune and hormonal systems.

PARTS USED:
ripe seeds (immature seeds can cause poisoning as they contain traces of prussic acid)

PROPERTIES/ACTIONS:
demulcent • antitussive • laxative • emollient • expectorant • detoxifying • anti-inflammatory

INDICATIONS:
gastritis • enteritis • colitis • catarrh • bronchitis • constipation • boils • shingles • psoriasis • coughs • burns and scalds • eczema • sprains and strains

CHAMOMILE *Matricaria recutita*

PARTS USED:
flowers

PROPERTIES/ACTIONS:
relaxant • anti-inflammatory • antispasmodic • anti-ulcer • astringent • anti-allergenic • digestive • antiseptic • diaphoretic • diuretic • decongestant • bitter tonic • painkilling • antifungal • antiviral

INDICATIONS:
inflammatory digestive problems • stress-related digestive problems • irritable bowel syndrome • gastritis • peptic ulcers • abdominal pain and spasm • catarrh • hay fever • eczema • asthma • headaches • leg ulcers • mastitis • hemorrhoids • heavy periods • depression • anxiety • insomnia • restlessness • diarrhea • poor appetite • heartburn • gall-bladder problems • urinary infections • fluid retention • muscle pain • sciatica • acne • tired eyes • styes • conjunctivitis • bruises • toothache • burns and scalds

Delicately fragrant, sedative and spirit-lifting, chamomile is a great healer for stress.

Chamomile is an all-time favourite when it comes to calming anxiety, soothing irritability, or combating nightmares. This gentle herb also relieves tension and inflammation in the digestive tract, making it wonderful for pain and colic, and for both constipation and diarrhea. Anti-inflammatory, anti-septic, and pain-relieving, chamomile will ease colds and flu, aches and pains, and a host of symptoms associated with infection or allergy, including cystitis and eczema. Use the tea as an antiseptic wash for wounds and thrush.

LEMON BALM *Melissa officinalis*

Once believed to hold a key to eternal life, lemon balm improves memory and aids concentration.

This lovely, relaxing herb, with its pleasant taste, will help to ease away headaches, migraines, insomnia and vertigo. Hot lemon-balm tea is antimicrobial and decongestant, wonderful for colds, flu, chest infections, and coughs, and one of the best remedies for the cold-sore virus. It will also help to lower fevers. Add a strong infusion to a child's bath to help calm over-excitement and induce restful sleep. Stress-related digestive problems, PMS, painful periods, anxiety, and depression all respond well to lemon balm.

PARTS USED:
leaves • flowers

PROPERTIES/ACTIONS:
diaphoretic • carminative • nervine • antispasmodic • antimicrobial • sedative • anti-emetic • antioxidant • decongestant • digestive • anti-allergenic • antiseptic • circulatory stimulant

INDICATIONS:
insomnia • stress-related problems • anxiety • colds • flu • asthma • fever • digestive problems • headaches • tiredness • nervous exhaustion • exam nerves • poor memory and concentration • depression • viral illnesses, such as herpes, shingles and mumps • PMS • coughs • earache • flatulence • urinary infections • cramp • urticaria • irregular periods • period pain

PEPPERMINT *Mentha piperita*

PARTS USED:
aerial parts

PROPERTIES/ACTIONS:
diaphoretic • carminative • nervine • antispasmodic • anti-emetic • antiseptic • digestive • circulatory stimulant • antimicrobial • bitter tonic • febrifuge • anti-inflammatory • relaxant • cholagogue • anesthetic • refrigerant • painkilling

INDICATIONS:
irritable bowel syndrome • gastritis • flatulence • nausea • catarrh • colds • flu • fever • poor circulation • headaches • stomach and bowel infections • diarrhea • halitosis • cramp • heartburn • arthritis • rheumatism • osteoporsis • bursitis and tendonitis • ringworm • herpes • scabies • head lice • cuts and wounds

Do not use mint on young babies; nor the oil on young children. Avoid if breast-feeding. Never apply the oil to the face or mucus membranes.

Warming and cooling, peppery and pungent, peppermint is the ultimate digestive.

Peppermint stimulates the flow of digestive juices. It is also a circulatory stimulant, promoting sweating and helping to overcome flu and fever. It helps to keep you warm in winter, yet cool in summer and, by increasing blood-flow to the brain, to keep the mind clear. Its decongestant properties help to clear catarrhal congestion. Try inhalations of the oil to clear the sinuses and relieve colds. In addition, from stomach gripes and indigestion to headaches and arthritis, peppermint will ease tension and pain.

BASIL *Ocimum basilicum*

Sweet basil can refresh you when you feel tired, and calm you when you feel tense or anxious.

If you are feeling stressed and exhausted, and suffering any of the related symptoms (headaches, indigestion, muscle tension, nerve pain, and so on), or you feel that your concentration or memory need a boost, basil will provide the tonic. The herb is both antiseptic and cleansing, helping the body to overcome all manner of infections. Hot basil tea reduces fevers and clears phlegm from the chest and nose, and so eases the symptoms of colds, flu, catarrh, coughs and sore throats. Its relaxant properties extend to both the digestive and respiratory tracts, and can relieve colic, constipation and nausea, and ease conditions such as asthma and tight coughs.

PARTS USED:
leaves

PROPERTIES/ACTIONS:
carminative • sedative • stomachic • antibacterial • anthelmintic • anti-depressant • antispasmodic • adrenal stimulant • febrifuge • diaphoretic • decongestant • peripheral vasodilator

INDICATIONS:
nervous irritability • poor concentration • nausea • vomiting • colic • constipation • depression • anxiety • fever • abdominal pain • infections • headaches • muscle tension • poor memory • nerve pain • catarrh • coughs • asthma • cuts and wounds • grazes • bites and stings • insomnia • flatulence • worms • head lice

EVENING PRIMROSE *Oenothera biennis*

PARTS USED:
oil from seeds • leaves • stems • flowers

PROPERTIES/ACTIONS:
astringent • anti-inflammatory • antispasmodic • digestive • immune-boosting • hormone-regulating • expectorant • cholesterol-lowering • hypotensive • anti-allergic • sedative

INDICATIONS:
eczema • hyperactivity • asthma • migraine • PMS • menopause • mild high blood pressure • intermittent claudication • high cholesterol • rheumatoid arthritis • MS • auto-immune problems • digestive problems • alcoholism • damaged liver • burns and scalds • bruises • nervous tension • sore throats

The elegant evening primrose provides great support for women's hormonal problems.

The oil of the evening-primrose seed contains GLA (gamma linoleic acid), a fatty acid that is vital for healthy functioning of both the immune system and the hormones. Try it if you are menopausal, or suffer from PMS. Evening primrose is also an excellent remedy for arthritis, auto-immune problems, and allergies. This healing herb can help to ease withdrawal symptoms from alcohol dependency and counteract the effects of excess alcohol on the liver. You can take the oil internally for skin problems, such as eczema.

GINSENG *Panax ginseng*

The king of all tonics, ginseng will boost your energy and protect against the effects of stress.

With its ability to enhance resistance to mental, emotional and physical stress, ginseng is a great herb for a modern world. The heart, circulation, hormones, and immune and nervous systems all benefit from a course of ginseng. The herb promotes overall physical and mental well-being, making it essential for the elderly or anyone recovering from illness. It has been particularly useful in enhancing the body's tolerance of cancer treatments. Ginseng also has aphrodisiac qualities, and can boost sperm production.

PARTS USED:
roots

PROPERTIES/ACTIONS:
adaptogen • general tonic • adrenal hormone stimulant • immune-boosting • antiviral • vasodilator • hypoglycemic • aphrodisiac • estrogenic

INDICATIONS:
ME/post-viral syndrome • exhaustion • stress • shingles • atherosclerosis • low libido • lowered immunity • convalescence • age-related problems • depression • poor concentration • osteoporosis • low sperm count

PASSIONFLOWER *Passiflora incarnata*

PARTS USED:
leaves

PROPERTIES/ACTIONS:
sedative • hypnotic • antispasmodic • diaphoretic • painkilling

INDICATIONS:
insomnia • restlessness • stress • irritability • anxiety • nerve pain • Parkinson's disease • nervous palpitations • asthma • shingles • coughs • toothache

This striking flower is a potent remedy to calm the spirit and induce restful sleep.

Passionflower is a wonderfully relaxing herb that has been known to bring on restorative and refreshing sleep, even in the most difficult cases of insomnia. It calms the nerves and gently soothes away muscle tension, making it perfect for relieving all kinds of stress-related problems. Passionflower has also been successful at easing nervous conditions such as shingles, neuralgia, and Parkinson's disease. If you suffer from asthma, or have a nervous cough, passionflower can help to relieve tension in the chest.

PARSLEY *Petroselinum crispum*

Since ancient times parsley has been used to enhance youth and beauty, and boost libido.

Parsley is packed with nutrients, notably vitamin C, which improves immunity and assists the body's absorption of iron, making this a good herb for anemia sufferers. Parsley stimulates the kidneys, helping to detoxify the body; and soothes the digestive tract, relieving conditions such as colic, indigestion and wind. Use a decoction of the seeds to ease abdominal cramps and headaches. Parsley can stimulate the uterine muscles; avoid it during pregnancy unless you want to use it to enhance contractions during childbirth.

PARTS USED:
roots • leaves • seeds

PROPERTIES/ACTIONS:
relaxant • antiseptic • general tonic • depurative • uterine tonic • diuretic • digestive • nervine • antirheumatic • antispasmodic

INDICATIONS:
flatulence • colic • menstrual problems • arthritis • urinary infections • poor circulation • exhaustion • anemia • poor appetite • indigestion • flatulence • headaches • migraines • asthma • fluid retention • gout • depression • anxiety • kidney stones • rheumatism • low libido • halitosis • cramp

Avoid taking parsley if you suffer from kidney disease.

PLANTAIN *Plantago major, Plantago psyllium*

PARTS USED:
leaves • seeds

PROPERTIES/ACTIONS:
anti-inflammatory • astringent • alterative • diuretic • vulnerary • demulcent • refrigerant • detoxifying • decongestant • expectorant • antiseptic • antispasmodic • laxative

INDICATIONS:
diarrhea • catarrh • allergies • gastritis • bronchitis • GI tract infections • urinary infections • boils • wounds • bites and stings • obesity • mouth ulcers • fluid retention • enlarged prostate • osteoporosis • eczema • acne • tired eyes • styes • burns and scalds

This unassuming leaf is great for combating inflammation and allergies.

If you suffer from eczema, acne or boils, plantain leaves will cool inflamed skin and expel toxins. Infections such as colds, sinusitis and earache, and conditions such as hay fever and asthma, respond well to hot plantain tea. The zinc-rich leaves can be helpful for an enlarged prostate, as well as stem bleeding, diarrhea and excessive menstruation. The plant's seeds (psyllium seeds) will bulk out stools, providing an excellent remedy for constipation or irritable bowel syndrome. Crush the fresh leaves as a topical first-aid treatment.

If you are on medication, do not eat the seeds for two hours before and after taking your medicine, as they can inhibit absorption.

ROSE *Rosa spp.*

The beautiful, sweet-smelling rose is the bloom of lovers – and also of well-being and longevity.

Rose leaves and petals can reduce fever, dispel toxins, boost immunity, and rebalance the bacterial population in the gut. If you are anxious, agitated, grieving or suffer from sleep problems, rose hips, petals and oil can all help to calm the mind and body, lift the mood, and promote restful sleep. A feminine flower, the rose has a special affinity for women, helping to relieve pelvic congestion and painful or heavy periods, and increase libido. Applied to the skin, rose water is wonderfully toning and cleansing.

PARTS USED:
hips • leaves • flowers

PROPERTIES/ACTIONS:
diaphoretic • carminative • general stimulant • emmenagogue • laxative • decongestant • febrifuge • nervine • anti-inflammatory • astringent • antimicrobial • thymoleptic • analgesic • detoxifying • hormone-regulating • antiseptic • antispasmodic • relaxant

INDICATIONS:
headaches • catarrh • GI tract infections • acidity • gastritis • acne • spots • depression • stress-related disorders • respiratory infections • period pain • PMS and other hormonal problems • inflammatory problems • insomnia • urticaria • fever • restlessness • impetigo • psoriasis • tired eyes • burns and scalds • toothache • nosebleeds

ROSEMARY *Rosmarinus officinalis*

PARTS USED:
leaves • twigs

PROPERTIES/ACTIONS:
antiseptic • antibacterial • antifungal • astringent • relaxant • memory-boosting • anti-ageing • antidepressive • anti-inflammatory • diuretic • stomachic • antispasmodic • diaphoretic • peripheral vasodilator • cholagogue • mild analgesic and parasiticide • uterine tonic • painkilling • antiviral

INDICATIONS:
headaches • migraines • arthritis • gout • fever • coughs • colds • sore throats • chest infections • asthma • poor memory and concentration • hangovers • poor circulation • depression • liver and gall-bladder problems • poor appetite • indigestion • insomnia • exhaustion • neuralgia • halitosis • fluid retention • rheumatism • bursitis and tendonitis • muscle pain • nerve pain • herpes • boils • scabies • head lice • bleeding gums • PMS • bruises • toothache

Deliciously aromatic, rosemary can banish negativity, dispel anxiety and lift the spirits.

Rosemary will strengthen the nerves, but soothe them too, making it wonderful if you are feeling low or anxious. The herb also stimulates the flow of blood to your head, improving mental clarity and concentration, and relieving headaches. Use the essential oil or take hot, rosemary tea to fight infections. Rosemary will stimulate the digestion, as well as promote the production of bile in the liver, and makes a great remedy for a hangover. A rosemary-oil massage will ease all manner of muscular or nerve pain.

SAGE *Salvia officinalis*

Sage's infection-fighting properties earned it the old name the of "herb of immortality".

Revered for thousands of years, sage is one of the most effective antimicrobial remedies for a cold, the flu, catarrh, a sore throat or a chest infection. It is an excellent digestive and bitter liver remedy, increasing digestion and the absorption of nutrients. Sage tea is a great diuretic, helping to clear the body of toxins and so useful in the treatment of arthritis and gout. Sage's estrogenic properties help to regulate periods, relieve period pain, and ease the symptoms of the menopause, particularly hot flushes.

PARTS USED:
leaves

PROPERTIES/ACTIONS:
carminative • antispasmodic • antiseptic • digestive • astringent • general tonic • antioxidant • rejuvenative • estrogenic • cholagogue • antibacterial • antiviral

INDICATIONS:
gingivitis • sore throats • mouth ulcers • laryngitis • pharyngitis • tonsillitis • wounds • indigestion • menopause • sweating • poor appetite • colds • chest infections • stomach and bowel infections • period pain • halitosis • osteoporosis • gout • arthritis • muscle pain • herpes • impetigo • irregular periods

Avoid taking sage during pregnancy and when breast-feeding.

ELDER *Sambucus nigra*

PARTS USED:
dried flowers • berries

PROPERTIES/ACTIONS:
diaphoretic • expectorant •
circulatory stimulant •
depurative • diuretic •
anti-inflammatory • diaphoretic •
diuretic • laxative • decongestant •
antioxidant

INDICATIONS:
colds • flu • chronic catarrh •
sinusitis • fever • eczema • hay
fever • acne • restlessness and
agitation • asthma • bronchitis •
chest infections • arthritis •
gout • laryngitis • tonsillitis •
acne • warts and verrucae •
conjunctivitis • tired eyes •
styes • burns and scalds

The elder tree is truly a pharmacy in itself, providing medicines for all manner of illness.

Early American settlers called the elder tree the "medicine chest of the people" as it can be used to treat such a wide range of ailments. Both the flowers and berries induce sweating and dispel toxins, clearing heat and inflammation from the body. The flowers alone are decongestant, anti-inflammatory and relaxant, and excellent for colds, flu and catarrh. The leaves, flowers, berries and bark are all diuretic. Elderberries are rich in immune-boosting vitamin C, and have a laxative effect.

SKULLCAP *Scutellaria lateriflora*

A member of the mint family, pretty skullcap makes an excellent tonic for the nerves.

Skullcap offers support for a busy, stressful life. Soothing and calming, skullcap can ease away anxiety, lift your mood and even relieve depression. If you feel tired or exhausted, skullcap will help to promote restful sleep. Combine skullcap with hormone-balancers, such as vitex, to reduce the symptoms of PMS or the menopause, and to help steady mood swings. The herb is also anti-inflammatory and painkilling. A hot cup of skullcap tea will reduce a fever.

PARTS USED:
leaves • flowers

PROPERTIES/ACTIONS:
nervine • sedative • antispasmodic • mild astringent • diuretic • thymoleptic • anti-inflammatory • painkilling

INDICATIONS:
nervous tension • PMS • depression • anxiety • insomnia • stress-related disorders • arthritis • headaches • period pain • palpitations • digestive disorders • fever • breast benign disorder • ME/post-viral syndrome • exhaustion • restlessness • muscle pain • nerve pain • toothache

MILK THISTLE *Silybum marianum*

PARTS USED:
seeds

PROPERTIES/ACTIONS:
cholagogue • galactagogue • demulcent • immune-boosting • detoxifying

INDICATIONS:
liver problems, including those related to alcohol abuse • poor milk-flow • gall-bladder problems • headaches • hangovers • poor digestion of fats • lethargy • hepatitis • acne • boils • PMS

If you live your life in the fast lane, protect your body with some nurturing milk thistle.

Headaches, early-morning lethargy, poor digestion of fatty foods, and dark, thick menstrual blood may all be signs that your liver is under pressure. Milk thistle is able to enhance the function of the liver and even regenerate liver-tissue, making it essential for anyone who has sustained liver damage, whether through disease (such as hepatitis), alcohol abuse, pollution or stress. The gall bladder is known to benefit, too. The plant is perfectly safe for breast-feeding mothers, who can use it to increase their flow of milk.

CHICKWEED *Stellaria media*

Pretty chickweed, with its white, star-shaped flowers, heralds the onset of spring.

Chickweed is a nutrient-rich herb, packed with vitamins A and C, and plenty of minerals, including iron. It has a light, refreshing taste – try eating it raw in salads. Apply cooling chickweed ointment to skin problems, such as eczema and sunburn, to speed healing and to relieve itching. It can calm inflammation in the gut and respiratory tract, making it good for gastritis, asthma and bronchitis. As a diuretic it helps to expel the toxins that exacerbate arthritis and gout. Apply the fresh leaves to scalds, bruises, ulcers and hemorrhoids.

PARTS USED:
leaves • flowers

PROPERTIES/ACTIONS:
antirheumatic • vulnerary • emollient • detoxifying • diuretic • anti-inflammatory

INDICATIONS:
cuts and wounds • eczema • psoriasis • boils • abscesses • acne • urticaria • impetigo • piles • ulcers • rheumatism • gout • arthritis • gastritis • sore throats • asthma • bronchitis • fluid retention • burns and scalds • hemorrhoids • anemia • bruises

⊕ ◉ ◐

DANDELION *Taraxacum officinale*

PARTS USED:
whole plant

PROPERTIES/ACTIONS:
digestive • bitter tonic • diuretic •
mild laxative • cholagogue •
alterative • painkilling •
detoxifying

INDICATIONS:
skin problems • arthritis • gout •
fluid retention • urinary
infections • indigestion • liver
and gall-bladder problems • warts
and verrucae • diabetes •
constipation • poor appetite •
heartburn • kidney stones •
anemia • rheumatism •
osteoporosis • eczema •
acne • PMS

A humble garden "weed", dandelion is a
remarkable detoxifier and liver tonic.

Dandelion has a bitter taste, which triggers the secretion of
digestive enzymes and bile from the liver. As a result dandelion helps to improve the appetite and digestion and
improves the action of the liver and gall bladder. Dandelion
root stimulates the pancreas, which secretes insulin, and so
can regulate blood sugar. Dandelion-leaf tea has a diuretic
action and makes a good wash for irritating skin complaints,
such as acne and eczema. Applied directly to the site of a
wart or verucca, the white "sap" can help to speed healing.

THYME *Thymus vulgaris*

Aromatic thyme will warm and invigorate you, and keep you youthful and full of energy.

If you are nervous, exhausted or depressed thyme can boost confidence, lift your mood and induce restful sleep. For adults and children alike, warming, gentle thyme is both expectorant and relaxant, and will help to soothe away bronchitis, pneumonia and other respiratory infections. Nervous coughs, asthma and even whooping cough can benefit, too. In the gut thyme will relieve spasm and fight infections. If you have candidiasis, or after antibiotics, thyme will help to rebalance the bacterial population in your bowel. Arthritis sufferers can benefit from thyme's diuretic properties, which help to expel toxins from the body. In lotions, apply thyme as a disinfectant for wounds, and to relieve muscular pain, and itching.

PARTS USED:
leaves • flowering tops

PROPERTIES/ACTIONS:
antiseptic • expectorant • diuretic • nervine • sedative • astringent • carminative • antioxidant • digestive tonic • anthelmintic • antitussive • detoxifying • antispasmodic • peripheral vasodilator • antiviral • antifungal • antibacterial • painkilling

INDICATIONS:
gastritis • bronchitis • asthma • whooping cough • diarrhea • indigestion • worms • tension • anxiety • colic • catarrh • laryngitis • tonsillitis • arthritis • gout • cuts and wounds • muscular pain • candidiasis • poor memory and concentration • colds • flu • sore throat • nausea and vomiting • halitosis • flatulence • osteoporosis • muscle pain • herpes • bleeding gums • toothache

❀ ♡ ◐ ◉ ◉

LIMEFLOWER *Tilia europaea*

PARTS USED:
flowers

PROPERTIES/ACTIONS:
nervine • antispasmodic • diaphoretic • diuretic • mild astringent • hypotensive • peripheral vasodilator

INDICATIONS:
stress-related illness, including depression • fever • catarrh • arthritis • gout • burns and scalds • red, inflamed eyes • colic • cramp • period pain • high blood pressure • arteriosclerosis • inflammatory skin problems • palpitations • restlessness

Also known as the linden flower, honey-scented limeflower comes from a tree loved by bees.

Symbolizing female beauty and grace, the linden tree gives us the perfect antidote to stress and stress-related illness, including headaches, tension and irritability. Taken as a tea, sweet-tasting limeflower helps to calm restlessness and induce sleep. If you suffer from coronary problems, lime-flower can relax the arteries, ease palpitations and reduce high blood pressure. The cooling properties of limeflower tea will help to chase away a fever. Apply the tea externally to ease the pain of burns and scalds.

RED CLOVER *Trifolium pratense*

Give yourself a spring clean with this deeply cleansing, wild herb with its cheerful red flower.

Red clover is diuretic and mildly laxative, helping to clear wastes through both the urinary and digestive systems. It also stimulates the liver, the body's built-in detoxifier. The flower is completely safe to give to both adults and children to help to ease conditions such as eczema and asthma. Red clover may be able to inhibit the growth of tumours, especially in female cancers, such as ovarian or breast cancer. It is also good for menopausal women: it helps to balance hormones and reduce symptoms such as hot flushes.

PARTS USED:
flowers

PROPERTIES/ACTIONS:
alterative • expectorant • antispasmodic • relaxant • diuretic • anti-inflammatory • hormone-regulating • antitumour • antiviral • antifungal • cholesterol-lowering • detoxifying • immune-boosting

INDICATIONS:
eczema • psoriasis • acne • impetigo • coughs • bronchitis • whooping cough • menopause • atherosclerosis • high cholesterol • asthma • irregular periods

NETTLE *Urtica dioica*

PARTS USED:
seeds • leaves of young plants • roots

PROPERTIES/ACTIONS:
antihemorrhagic • diuretic • astringent • restorative • galactagogue • detoxifying • anti-inflammatory • antispasmodic

INDICATIONS:
rheumatism • heavy periods • menopause • anemia • eczema • exhaustion • catarrh • enlarged prostate • hair loss • hay fever • asthma • nosebleeds • catarrh • ulcers • dandruff • bleeding gums • cuts and wounds • urinary infections • fluid retention • osteoporosis • gout • sciatica • acne • urticaria • boils • impetigo • sunburn

The much-maligned common stinging nettle is one of the most versatile herbal remedies of all.

From kidney stones to the menopause, the humble nettle provides a remedy. The leaves and stems are packed with vitamins and minerals, including vitamins A and C, and potassium, iron and calcium, and make a good remedy for allergies; the roots can prevent hair loss and help reduce an enlarged prostate. The diuretic action of nettle tea helps to clear toxins from the body, while its astringency will help to stem bleeding, lessen diarrhea and heal ulcers. Even the sting, which brings blood to the surface of the skin, helps to relieve joint pain and swelling.

Always use gloves when handling raw nettles; and never eat them raw.

BILBERRY *Vaccinium myrtillus*

Delicious, blue fruits, bilberries burst with nutrients to keep us young and healthy.

Bilberries contain antioxidants that help to repair environmental damage to our skin, and help to prevent the degenerative symptoms of the ageing process; tannins that help to protect the digestive, urinary and respiratory systems from infection; and vitamins A and C, bioflavonoids, and iron. The fruits are also antiviral and antifungal, and have an antibiotic effect in the urinary tract. Try bilberry juice for a fever or for inflammation; or a bilberry mouthwash for mouth ulcers or a sore throat.

PARTS USED:
berries • leaves

PROPERTIES/ACTIONS:
antibacterial • antiviral • diuretic • diaphoretic • antioxidant • astringent

INDICATIONS:
eye problems • fever • bleeding gums • mouth ulcers • hemorrhoids • sore throats • intestinal inflammation • gout • rheumatoid arthritis • varicose veins • urinary infections • irritable bowel syndrome • kidney stones • anemia • varicose ulcers

Bilberries can cause allergic reactions in some people.

✿ ◗ ✤ 🌍 ❤ ✳

VERVAIN *Verbena officinalis*

PARTS USED:
leaves • flowers

PROPERTIES/ACTIONS:
nervine • antidepressant • relaxant • cholagogue • febrifuge • galactagogue • emmenagogue • diuretic • antispasmodic • anti-inflammatory • digestive

INDICATIONS:
depression • exhaustion • anxiety • tension • migraines • headaches • fever • gum disease • water retention • urinary infections • eczema • PMS • stress-related period pain • high blood pressure • insomnia • nightmares

A delicate plant, with pretty mauve flowers, vervain is a great friend in times of stress.

Almost all forms of stress and stress-related symptoms can benefit from vervain's relaxing and mood-lifting properties. If you suffer from PMS, try vervain to lift your spirits and reduce period pain. Vervain is quite a bitter herb and so is good for the digestive system, stimulating the flow of gastric juices and enhancing the absorption of nutrients. It also enhances liver and gall-bladder function. Hot vervain tea can reduce a fever. Taken cool the tea can clear bacteria from the urinary tract, making it a good remedy for cystitis.

VITEX *Vitex agnus-castus*

Also known as the chasteberry, vitex is a sweet-scented berry, and a great remedy for women.

Vitex has a simply amazing ability to regulate the hormones, making it the best remedy for period pain, PMS, and a range of gynecological complaints, including fibroids, endometriosis, and ovarian cysts. It is also excellent for fertility problems, painful or swollen breasts, and the symptoms of the menopause. In women who are breast-feeding, vitex can help to promote a good supply of milk. In men vitex is often able to cool sexual passion, a property that has given rise to its nickname, "monk's pepper".

PARTS USED:
berries

PROPERTIES/ACTIONS:
uterine tonic • galactagogue • hormone-regulating • antispasmodic • relaxant

INDICATIONS:
overactive/low libido • menstrual cramps • PMS • ovarian cysts • endometriosis • poor milk-flow • menopause • period pain • fibroids • irregular periods • breast pain • enlarged prostate

ASHWAGANDHA *Withania somnifera*

PARTS USED:

roots

PROPERTIES/ACTIONS:

sedative • nervine • rejuvenative • anti-inflammatory • antitumour • adaptogen • antioxidant • immune-boosting • painkilling • antimicrobial • antispasmodic • reproductive stimulant

INDICATIONS:

exhaustion • nervousness • insomnia • lowered immunity • digestive problems • arthritis • skin problems • coughs • asthma • anxiety • fever • auto-immune disorders • hay fever • insomnia • panic attacks • low libido • fertility problems, including low sperm count • depression • restlessness • rheumatism • muscle pain • MS

Known as "Indian Ginseng", Ashwagandha increases energy and induces calm.

Ashwagandha is a must for anyone with a busy, stressful life. Use it to strengthen your reserves and reduce all the telltale signs of stress, such as insomnia and exhaustion. The herb is both rejuvenative and antioxidant, helping to speed recovery from illness. Its sedative properties can help to calm children with behavioural problems. As an immune-booster, ashwagandha can be given in auto-immune diseases such as multiple sclerosis and rheumatoid arthritis. Both women and men can use ashwagandha to boost fertility and libido.

GINGER *Zingiber officinale*

A stimulant for the heart and circulation, ginger provides an overall boost to well-being.

Drinking a cup of hot, fresh ginger tea at the onset of a cold or flu will help you to "sweat out" the infection, reduce fever and clear catarrh. The spice is well known as a remedy for all manner of gastric upsets, including diarrhea, griping pain and stomach spasms. If you suffer from travel sickness, ginger will help to ease nausea, and it is also safe to use during pregnancy for morning sickness. Its warming properties stimulate the circulation, invigorate the digestion, and dispel lethargy. Chewing on fresh ginger can relieve toothache.

PARTS USED:
rhizomes

PROPERTIES/ACTIONS:
carminative • diuretic • aphrodisiac • thermogenic • emollient • appetizer • antioxidant • laxative • stomachic • general stimulant • anthelmintic • antitussive • anti-emetic • rubefacient • diaphoretic • antispasmodic • anti-inflammatory • expectorant • antiseptic • reproductive stimulant • circulatory stimulant • anesthetic • tissue-healing • antifungal • detoxifying

INDICATIONS:
poor appetite • coughs • colds • flu • catarrh • arthritis • inflammation • nausea • vomiting • asthma • fever • constipation • indigestion • diarrhea • flatulence • poor circulation • chilblains • cramp • raised cholesterol • poor absorption • heartburn • anemia • rheumatism • bursitis and tendonitis • muscle pain • sciatica • ringworm • low libido • irregular periods • bruises • sprains and strains

THE NERVOUS SYSTEM

001 POOR CONCENTRATION

Stress, tiredness, nutritional deficiencies, digestive problems and food intolerances can all cause poor concentration. Optimize your diet – eat lots of the vitamins and minerals that aid brain function (particularly iron, zinc, B-vitamins, magnesium and essential fatty acids), and cut out the additives and stimulants (colourings, flavourings, caffeine and so on) that hinder it. Herbal treatments can reduce stress, promote concentration, and aid the absorption of essential nutrients into the body. Finally, try to live a balanced life: make time for relaxation as well as work.

USEFUL HERBS: Skullcap (p.57), Vervain (p.66), Wild oats (p.25), Licorice (p.39), Gotu cola (p.27), Rosemary (p.54), Lemon balm (p.45), Lavender (p.42), Basil (p.47), Coriander (p.30), Ashwagandha (p.68), Thyme (p.61), Ginseng (p.49), Ginger (p.69)

TREATMENTS:

- To minimize stress, drink teas or standard-dose tinctures of adaptogen herbs, including ashwagandha, licorice, wild oats, ginseng, vervain and skullcap, three times a day.
- To improve alertness and concentration, and to enhance brain function, drink teas or tinctures of gotu cola and thyme, three times a day.
- Take teas of rosemary, lemon balm, lavender or basil to still an overactive mind.
- Aid the absorption of nutrients and increase mental alertness by using lots of coriander and ginger in your cooking.

002 POOR MEMORY

If our mind becomes overloaded, perhaps through stress or illness, or if we are lacking in certain nutrients or there is an imbalance in our hormones (such as during the menopause or as a result of low thyroid activity), our memory may start to malfunction. Many people associate forgetfulness with the ageing process. A decline in mental function during old age generally begins with short-term memory loss. Pack your diet full with B-vitamins, choline, lecithin, antioxidants (found in foods rich in vitamins C and E, including fruit, vegetable, nuts and seeds), and essential fatty acids, which are all vital for boosting your short-term memory. Supplements of coenzyme Q10, zinc and selenium will help, too.

USEFUL HERBS: Bilberry (p.65), Rosemary (p.54), Thyme (p.61), Lemon balm (p.45), Gotu cola (p.27), Wild oats (p.25), Ashwagandha (p.68)

TREATMENTS:

- Take gotu cola regularly as a standard-dose tincture. This herb has an amazing ability to improve the flow of blood (and so the supply of oxygen) to the brain and in turn improve overall brain function, including short-term memory.
- Take regular teas or standard-dose tinctures of antioxidant-rich herbs, such as rosemary, thyme, ashwagandha and lemon balm, which help to protect the nervous system from damage by free radicals; and wild oats, which act as tonics to the nervous system.

003 TENSION AND ANXIETY

It is quite normal to feel anxious or tense in a stressful situation. However, if our nervous system becomes depleted through long-term stress, or through illness or a poor diet, we may suffer from a generalized feeling of tension or anxiety with no particular cause. We can develop stress-related physical symptoms, such as stomach and bowel problems, high blood pressure, allergies, and skin problems. A healthy diet will help to support us through difficult times: eat plenty of fresh, organic fruit and vegetables, and avoid caffeine, sugar, alcohol, and any unnecessary drugs, which can hamper our ability to cope with stress. Take plenty of exercise.

USEFUL HERBS: Vervain (p.66), Skullcap (p.57), Wild oats (p.25), Ginseng (p.49), Chamomile (p.44), Hops (p.40), Passionflower (p.50), Lemon balm (p.45), Lavender (p.42), Limeflower (p.62), Ashwagandha (p.68), Gotu cola (p.27), Wild yam (p.32), Thyme (p.61)

TREATMENTS:
- Take teas or standard-dose tinctures of nerve tonics (gotu cola, lavender, vervain, skullcap, wild oats, ashwagandha and ginseng) to calm and strengthen you and improve your resilience.
- To relax combine wild oats and skullcap in a standard tincture three to six times a day.
- To ease muscle tension and soothe anxiety, have a relaxing massage using 2 drops of the essential oils of lavender, basil, rosemary, rose or chamomile diluted in 1 tsp sesame oil.

004 DEPRESSION

Whether the cause is physical, environmental or emotional, depression is a debilitating illness that comes with feelings of powerlessness, hopelessness, sorrow and anger, and symptoms such as insomnia and poor concentration. Left untreated depression can last for several months, even years. Studies suggest that twice as many women as men have severe depression. One reason might be that the hormone estrogen is a mild antidepressant, but in menopausal women estrogen levels fall, and some women become depressed. To help relieve depression, eat healthily, and exercise regularly to release feel-good hormones.

USEFUL HERBS: Vervain (p.66), Skullcap (p.57), Rosemary (p.54), Parsley (p.51), Basil (p.47), Ginseng (p.49), Chamomile (p.44), Rose (p.53), Ashwagandha (p.68), Lemon balm (p.45), Lavender (p.42), Gotu cola (p.27), Wild oats (p.25), Licorice (p.39)

TREATMENTS:
- Take adaptogen herbs (licorice, wild oats, gotu cola, ginseng and ashwagandha) as teas or standard-dose tinctures three times a day; they will lift the spirits and boost resilience to stress.
- Take teas of basil, vervain, lemon balm or skullcap, individually or in combination, three to six times a day to brighten your mood.
- Add the oil of rose, lavender or rosemary to your baths, or 2 drops to 1 tsp sesame oil for a massage, to lift the spirits and reduce tension.

THE NERVOUS SYSTEM

THE NERVOUS SYSTEM

005 INSOMNIA

Restorative sleep is vital to our well-being and yet around one third of adults develop insomnia at one time or another. Whatever the cause of insomnia (whether it is a result of stress and anxiety or some social or nutritional factor, such as shift-work or a poor diet), try not to become anxious about your lack of sleep, and instead take positive steps to overcome it. Cut out caffeine, alcohol and tobacco, and try an early-morning walk to reset your body clock. Take 45 minutes' quiet time before bed to ensure that your mind is calm and free from the stresses of the day before trying to sleep.

USEFUL HERBS: Chamomile (p.44), Lemon balm (p.45), Hops (p.40), Skullcap (p.57), Passionflower (p.50), Lavender (p.42), Ashwagandha (p.68), Basil (p.47), Rosemary (p.54), Wild oats (p.25), Vervain (p.66), Rose (p.53)

TREATMENTS:

• Throughout the evening and just before bed, take teas of chamomile, basil and lavender to help calm you and ease you into restful sleep.

• Every night before bed try taking 1–3 tsp of a combination of passionflower and skullcap tinctures, diluted in a little water.

• Before bed massage your body (or at least the soles of your feet) with warm sesame oil. Wait ten to 15 minutes and then have a warm bath laced with a few drops of diluted, relaxing essential oils, such as lavender, basil or rose.

006 HEADACHE AND MIGRAINE

At one time or another we all suffer from headaches. Both headaches and migraines (which are often accompanied by feelings of nausea and dizziness) can come on as a result of dehydration, stress, tiredness, allergy, hormonal problems, or even pollution; or because of illnesses such as colds, flu or sinusitis. Learn to understand what triggers your headaches (and avoid those triggers) and be aware that the headaches may be a symptom of a variety of medical conditions, which you need to identify. Avoid caffeine, sugar and alcohol, as well as known migraine triggers, such as chocolate, cheese, and citrus fruits.

USEFUL HERBS: Elder (p.56), Meadowsweet (p.36), Rosemary (p.54), Gotu cola (p.27), Vervain (p.66), Chamomile (p.44), Lavender (p.42), Milk thistle (p.58), Basil (p.47), Peppermint (p.46)

TREATMENTS:

• If you are prone to frequent headaches take teas or standard-dose tinctures of meadowsweet, gotu cola, vervain or rosemary, either individually or in combination, three times a day for two or three weeks.

• If a headache threatens it is important to take your herbal remedy as soon as possible. Teas of rosemary, ginger and gotu cola will often stop a headache in its tracks.

• Using your middle fingers, gently massage your temples with a few drops of basil, rosemary or peppermint oil.

007 TIREDNESS AND EXHAUSTION

Whether as a result of age, pollution, overwork, chronic stress, or a poor diet, tiredness and exhaustion can be extremely frustrating, and sometimes debilitating. To boost your vitality eat a healthy diet full of the antioxidant vitamins A, C and E, as well as B-vitamins, and iron, calcium and magnesium. Supplements of vitamin C, coenzyme Q10, and zinc will also help to boost your energy levels. Try lowering your intake of refined carbohydrates, which can make you feel lethargic, and avoid eating refined foods, sugar and saturated fats, and drinking alcohol and caffeine.

USEFUL HERBS:
Vervain (p.66), Cinnamon (p.29), Licorice (p.39), Skullcap (p.57), Wild oats (p.25), Echinacea (p.33), Nettle (p.64), Lavender (p.42), Rosemary (p.54), Ginseng (p.49), Gotu cola (p.27), Ashwagandha (p.68), Ginger (p.69)

TREATMENTS:

- Nourishing herbs, such as wild oats, ginseng, gotu cola, licorice and ashwagandha, taken three times a day as powders, teas or standard-dose tinctures, will strengthen and energize you.
- Begin the day with freshly grated ginger root in a cup of boiling water, to stimulate your digestion and ensure that you optimize your nutrient-intake from your food.
- If you feel exhausted by illness, take echinacea or cinnamon, three times a day, as teas, standard-dose tinctures, or powders.

008 RESTLESSNESS AND AGITATION

Inevitably in life we will suffer from periods of restlessness and agitation. However, prolonged agitation can deplete our vital energy and lead to illness. Support your nervous system with a nutritious diet containing plenty of essential fatty acids, vitamins B and C, and the minerals zinc, potassium, calcium, magnesium and iron. Avoid caffeine, excess alcohol, smoking, and a diet high in sugar and refined carbohydrates, which deplete your nervous system.

USEFUL HERBS: Passionflower (p.50), Skullcap (p.57), Ashwagandha (p.68), Chamomile (p.44), Vervain (p.66), Lemon balm (p.45), Wild oats (p.25), Licorice (p.39), Lavender (p.42), Rosemary (p.54), Rose (p.53), Basil (p.47), Limeflower (p.62), Hops (p.40)

TREATMENTS:

- Strengthen your nervous system by taking teas or standard-dose tinctures of ginseng, ashwagandha, licorice, skullcap, wild oats, rosemary, vervain or lemon balm, individually or in combinations, three times a day.
- To calm acute restlessness or agitation, take teas or standard-dose tinctures of lavender, passionflower, skullcap, rose, chamomile, basil, limeflower and hops, individually or combined, up to every two hours throughout the day.
- Induce calm by using a few drops of lavender, chamomile, basil, rose or rosemary essential oil in baths or burners, or as perfumes.

THE NERVOUS SYSTEM

009 NEURALGIA

Neuralgia is the intense pain associated with an inflamed or injured nerve, and most common among people who suffer from sciatica, lumbago or trigeminal neuralgia (a condition that affects the trigeminal nerve, which serves the face). Apart from physical causes – such as accidents or a slipped disk – excess alcohol, diabetes and the toxic influence of heavy metals such as lead or mercury can also traumatize the nerves. Recovery relies upon properly identifying the source of the pain, so if you experience neuralgia always consult an osteopath or chiropractor.

USEFUL HERBS: Ginger (p.69), Lavender (p.42), Wild oats (p.25), Vervain (p.66), Licorice (p.39), Skullcap (p.57), Wild yam (p.32), Passionflower (p.50), Black cohosh (p.28), Echinacea (p.33), Peppermint (p.46), Chamomile (p.44), Ashwagandha (p.68), Rosemary (p.54)

TREATMENTS:
- Eat plenty of wild oats, which will help to repair nerve tissue.
- To ease the pain take ½ tsp black cohosh and passionflower tincture three to six times a day.
- To relieve pain and inflammation, rub a little ashwagandha or gotu cola oil into the area.
- If stress is contributing to your pain, take teas or standard-dose tinctures of relaxing herbs such as ashwagandha, gotu cola, lemon balm, chamomile, skullcap or vervain, three to six times a day.

010 SHINGLES

An inflammatory nerve disease, shingles is caused by the varicella zoster virus (a type of herpes), which also causes chicken pox. A skin rash appears along the site of a nerve, and brings with it a tingling sensation and intense pain. You are more likely to succumb to shingles after contact with chicken pox (the virus lies dormant in the system and reactivates as shingles), and also if your immune system is run-down. During infection try to avoid eating foods that inhibit immunity and stimulate inflammation, such as saturated fats, refined foods and sugars, and caffeine and alcohol. Take supplements of beta-carotene, zinc and vitamins C and E, which will enhance your immunity and help to heal the skin; and of calcium, magnesium, and B-complex vitamins to support the nervous system.

USEFUL HERBS: Lemon balm (p.45), Lavender (p.42), Skullcap (p.57), Wild oats (p.25), Vervain (p.66), Licorice (p.39), Echinacea (p.33), Burdock (p.24), Chamomile (p.44), Marigold (p.26), Gotu cola (p.27), Ashwagandha (p.68)

TREATMENTS:
- To fight the virus take teas or standard-dose tinctures of echinacea, licorice, burdock, lemon balm or chamomile, three to six times a day.
- To reduce pain and inflammation, take teas or standard-dose tinctures of skullcap, vervain and gotu cola.
- Take frequent teas or standard-dose tinctures of passionflower and lavender to help relieve the pain during and after infection.

011 ACNE

Hormonal imbalances, particularly during adolescence, can cause the sebaceous gland (which secretes sebum, the skin's natural moisturizer) to become overactive, giving us oily skin, especially on the face, back and chest. The increased sebum blocks the hair follicles, causing the acne spots. To keep your skin clear avoid fatty foods and dairy produce, high-sugar foods, red meat, and caffeine. Fresh fruit and vegetables, and supplements of zinc, cod-liver oil and B-complex vitamins will help to keep the skin healthy.

USEFUL HERBS: Burdock (p.24), Milk thistle (p.58), Chamomile (p.44), Rose (p.53), Echinacea (p.33), Marigold (p.26), Plantain (p.52), Elder (p.56), Chickweed (p.59), Cleavers (p.38), Dandelion (p.60), Red clover (p.63), Nettle (p.64), Coriander (p.30), Hawthorn (p.31)

TREATMENTS:

• Instead of using soap (which washes away the acid mantle of the skin, making it prone to infection), clean your face every day with rose water, chamomile or elderflower water, or fine oatmeal mixed with a little water.

• Each morning apply marigold cream, which is soothing, detoxifying and antiseptic.

• To help clear heat and inflammation from the skin, drink teas made using detoxifying herbs, such as milk thistle, dandelion root, cleavers, nettles and red clover, individually or in combination, three to six times a day.

012 BOILS AND ABSCESSES

A boil is a hard, tender swelling that arises when staphylococcal bacteria cause an infection in the hair roots and sweat glands. As the pus-filled lumps make their way to the surface of the skin they come to a head, and usually burst after a few days. Boils tend to indicate an overheated, congested, rather toxic state of the body, which can result from poor diet, constipation, lack of exercise, and poor fat metabolism. Never squeeze a boil – allow it to surface and burst naturally. However, a hot poultice can speed up this process.

USEFUL HERBS: Marsh mallow (p.23), Dandelion (p.60), Milk thistle (p.58), Burdock (p.24), Echinacea (p.33), Nettle (p.64), Licorice (p.39), Linseed (p.43), Plantain (p.52), Rosemary (p.54), Chickweed (p.59), Cleavers (p.38)

TREATMENTS:

• To help a boil to surface, apply a hot poultice for an hour three times a day. Use linseed, plantain, chickweed, marsh mallow or burdock.

• To help fight infection and clear inflammation, take ¼–½ tsp echinacea tincture three to six times a day.

• To help the liver detoxify the body, take teas of liver herbs, such as dandelion root, burdock or rosemary, three times a day.

• To ensure that the bowels are clear, soak 1 or 2 tsp linseeds in water for two hours and then drink the mixture just before bed; or, take a nightcap of dandelion root and licorice tea.

THE SKIN AND EYES

THE SKIN AND EYES

013 HERPES

A highly contagious virus, and a relative of varicella zoster (which causes shingles), herpes simplex shows itself in our bodies in two different ways: cold sores (sometimes called fever blisters) and genital herpes. Cold sores generally develop around the mouth, and especially on the lips, although they can appear anywhere on the face, and even the hands. You are more likely to develop a cold sore when your immunity is low – such as when you are tired and run-down, stressed, or coming down with an infection. In women genital herpes occurs in and around the vagina and on the cervix. In men it develops on and around the penis. It can also occur around the anus. The genital form of the condition is usually transmitted through sexual contact, but can also occur as a result of cross-infection, by touching the mouth and then the genitals. Both kinds of herpes simplex cause a tingling, burning or itching sensation, followed by raised red areas that develop into painful, fluid-filled blisters. Once the blisters have burst, they will begin to heal. Cold sores will usually be gone within seven to ten days; genital herpes may take several weeks. The virus remains dormant until activated again.

Exposure to the sun, wind or cold and lowered immunity can all trigger a cold sore, but so can a poor diet. To try to inhibit the virus, eat a diet that is low in the amino acid arginine (found in such foods as chocolate and peanuts) and high in lysine (star fruits, papayas, grapefruits, apricots, pears, apples and figs). Cystine, another amino acid, will also help to prevent the virus flaring up – it is found in watercress, black beans, lentils, and soya beans. Vitamin-C supplements, and supplements of zinc and quercetin, all fight the herpes simplex virus. A really good trick for the first sign of a cold sore is to apply a cooled, wet teabag

(Darjeeling or Assam are best as they are particularly rich in tannic acid, which has strong antiviral properties) to the tingle, several times a day.

USEFUL HERBS: Lemon balm (p.45), Peppermint (p.46), Echinacea (p.33), Rosemary (p.54), Sage (p.55), Thyme (p.61), Garlic (p.21), Licorice (p.39), Burdock (p.24), Marigold (p.26), Elecampane (p.41)

TREATMENTS:

- Licorice deactivates the herpes simplex virus and is a great anti-inflammatory. Take it internally as a tea or ½ tsp tincture three times daily, and apply licorice cream to the site.
- At the first signs take ½ tsp echinacea tincture every 2 hours. Dab a little echinacea onto the cold-sore site to numb the pain.
- Lemon balm has strong antiviral effects. Apply the oil or freshly bruised leaves to the herpes site, or bathe the area with strong lemon-balm tea (4 tsp per cup boiling water) several times a day. Drinking the tea will also help.
- Rosemary, thyme and peppermint also have antiviral properties. Apply the cooled tea to the herpes site several times a day. Again, drinking cups of the hot tea will also help.
- Boost your overall immunity by taking raw garlic, or garlic capsules, three times daily.

014 URTICARIA AND HIVES

Urticaria is an allergic skin condition that causes a red rash, which may be itchy, often accompanied by joint pain. Certain foods, including citrus fruits, milk, nuts, strawberries, chocolate, shellfish, artificial colourings, and foods high in salicylates (such as grapes, dried fruits, and tomatoes), will often trigger the reaction; as will certain substances, such as animal dander, pollen, make-up, insect stings, and even strong sunlight.

USEFUL HERBS: Burdock (p.24), Chickweed (p.59), Licorice (p.39), Aloe vera (p.22), Milk thistle (p.58), Chamomile (p.44), Rose (p.53), Lemon balm (p.45), Echinacea (p.33), Marigold (p.26), Nettle (p.64), Coriander (p.30), Yarrow (p.20)

TREATMENTS:

- To relieve itching and inflammation in an acute reaction, soak in a warm herbal bath made with double-strength (use twice as much herb as standard) teas of burdock and chickweed.
- Also for itching and inflammation, apply aloe vera juice to the area, or bathe it with rose or marigold water, or the juice of fresh coriander leaves (liquidize the leaves with a little water).
- Take anti-allergenic teas of lemon balm, nettle, chamomile or yarrow three to six times daily.
- To support the immune system and clear heat from the skin, take echinacea, chamomile and a little licorice and milk thistle tincture three times daily.

015 IMPETIGO

Impetigo is a bacterial infection of the skin (usually caused by the staphylococcal or streptococcal bacteria) that starts as a rash of small, fluid-filled blisters, which then scab over. If your skin is already upset in some way, perhaps by eczema or a cold sore, impetigo can develop as a secondary infection. It tends to affect the area around the lips, nose and ears and is highly contagious. To avoid spreading the infection, try not to touch the affected area, and keep the infected person's towels, facecloths and bed linen separate from those of other members of the household.

USEFUL HERBS: Echinacea (p.33), Marigold (p.26), Lavender (p.42), Thyme (p.61), Rose (p.53), Chickweed (p.59), Red clover (p.63), Nettle (p.64), Garlic (p.21), Sage (p.55), Cleavers (p.38), Burdock (p.24)

TREATMENTS:

- Bathe the affected area with lavender water or rose water, or with infusions of lavender or rose, every day as often as you can.
- Combat the infection by taking teas of antibacterial herbs, such as echinacea, marigold, thyme or sage, three times a day.
- Take raw garlic, or garlic capsules, two or three times daily to help to clear the infection.
- If you suffer regular skin infections, or are predisposed to them, take cleavers, nettles, chickweed, and red clover three times daily to help to clear your system of heat and toxins.

THE SKIN AND EYES

016 WARTS AND VERUCCAE

A wart is caused by the papilloma virus, which triggers the overproduction of skin cells. These cells die and group together as a small, hard, benign growth on the surface of the skin. A verucca is the name often given to a wart on the foot. Most warts tend not to be painful, although veruccae on the soles of the feet can cause some discomfort. Warts will often appear on warm, moist areas of the body, such as the palms of the hands, and are particularly contagious in damp areas, such as bathrooms and swimming pools. A wart will eventually disappear on its own, although it may take months or even years. You can speed up the process with persistent treatment using herbs.

USEFUL HERBS: Dandelion (p.60), Elder (p.56), Burdock (p.24), Echinacea (p.33), Red clover (p.63), Licorice (p.39), Garlic (p.21), Marigold (p.26)

TREATMENTS:
- Squeeze the stem of a dandelion and apply the white juice to the wart or verruca every day for as long as the lesion persists. Elderberry juice and the yellow sap of greater celandine have similar effects and make good alternatives.
- Enhance your immunity to the papilloma virus, and clear toxins from your system, by drinking teas or standard-dose tinctures of burdock, dandelion root, echinacea, and red clover, with a little licorice, three times a day.
- Garlic has effective antiviral properties. Take it raw or in a capsule every day.

017 RINGWORM AND ATHLETE'S FOOT

Ringworm is caused by a fungus that feeds off keratin, a substance found in the uppermost layer of our skin, hair and nails. The infection usually appears as small, circular, itchy lesions and is highly contagious, especially in warm, damp conditions, such as bathrooms and swimming pools. When ringworm appears on the feet it is known as athlete's foot. In chronic cases athlete's foot can affect the toenails, causing them to become thick and yellow. To prevent ringworm spreading use separate towels and wash your hands after touching infected areas.

USEFUL HERBS: Aloe vera (p.22), Chamomile (p.44), Burdock (p.24), Thyme (p.61), Marigold (p.26), Garlic (p.21), Rosemary (p.54), Rose (p.53), Cinnamon (p.29), Ginger (p.69), Peppermint (p.46)

TREATMENTS:
- Take antifungal, digestive teas, including thyme, marigold, chamomile, burdock, rose, cinnamon or ginger, three times a day.
- To help establish the normal bacterial population of the gut, take 25ml (1 fl. oz) aloe vera juice, morning and night.
- For athlete's foot soak your feet twice a day in strong teas of marigold, thyme, cinnamon, ginger, peppermint or chamomile.
- Apply marigold or chamomile cream to the ringworm two or three times a day.
- Take garlic raw or in capsules every day.

018 SCABIES

Characterized by intense itching and small, fluid-filled blisters, scabies is caused by tiny parasites. The female mite embeds herself just under the surface of the skin to lay her eggs. The condition is highly contagious. When the eggs hatch we can catch them easily by direct contact or from bed linen or clothing (where they can survive for about two weeks), or from pets. You can get scabies anywhere on the skin, but you are more likely to get it between the fingers, on the hands, wrists or elbows, in the armpits, or on the genitals or feet. The itching is aggravated by warmth and so tends to be worse in bed. Follow the three-step procedure below to get rid of the scabies, and try not to scratch as this may cause a secondary infection.

USEFUL HERBS: Echinacea (p.33), Lavender (p.42), Rosemary (p.54), Peppermint (p.46), Garlic (p.21), Elecampane (p.41)

TREATMENTS:

- Add antimicrobial herbs in strong teas to a hot bath at night and soak for at least ten minutes. Thyme, marigold, lavender, peppermint, rosemary, rose, burdock or echinacea are all good herbs to use.
- Dry yourself vigorously. Dilute 2 drops of the essential oil of any of the bath herbs in 1 tsp sesame oil and apply the mixture to your skin.
- Go to bed in clean nightclothes. Hot-wash and iron your bed linen the following day. Repeat the whole process for two more nights.

019 ECZEMA

Eczema has many triggers and proper treatment depends upon knowing what your trigger is. For many people the condition is the result of an overactive immune system resulting in an allergy to such things as animal dander, dust mites, or certain foods (especially dairy products and wheat). You can help to relieve the condition by eating a healthy diet that is rich in essential fatty acids, and in essential vitamins and nutrients, including vitamins A, B, C and E and the minerals zinc, magnesium, calcium and iron. Stress will exacerbate eczema, so try to find time to relax.

USEFUL HERBS: Chamomile (p.44), Licorice (p.39), Echinacea (p.33), Yarrow (p.20), Vervain (p.66), Dandelion (p.60), Evening primrose (p.48), Linseed (p.43), Red clover (p.63), Burdock (p.24), Aloe vera (p.22), Cleavers (p.38), Plantain (p.52), Elder (p.56), Chickweed (p.59), Nettle (p.64)

TREATMENTS:

- Soothing chamomile is probably the best herb of all for allergic skin conditions. Drink a cup of chamomile tea, three to six times a day. You can also dilute 2 drops chamomile essential oil in 1 tsp coconut oil and apply it to the skin.
- For hot, inflamed skin, drink cooling teas of red clover, dandelion leaf, and burdock individually or combined, three to six times a day.
- For dry, itching skin, apply a little linseed oil or evening primrose oil to the area, and take a 500mg evening-primrose-oil supplement daily.

THE SKIN AND EYES

THE SKIN AND EYES

020 PSORIASIS

Psoriasis is an auto-immune disorder that affects the skin, causing patches of redness, with dry, silvery scales. The condition most commonly affects the elbows, ears, knees, legs, scalp and lower back, although it can also affect the fingernails, causing them to become yellowed and brittle. The precise causes of psoriasis are uncertain, although depleted immunity as a result of high levels of stress or shock, poor nutrition and food allergy or intolerance are all thought to be triggers. Sunlight can help to heal psoriasis, so spend some time outdoors; and take supplements of zinc, selenium, and vitamin E to support your immune system.

USEFUL HERBS: Burdock (p.24), Cleavers (p.38), Licorice (p.39), Linseed (p.43), Chickweed (p.59), Red clover (p.63), Ashwagandha (p.68), Marigold (p.26), Evening primrose (p.48), Rose (p.53), Aloe vera (p.22)

TREATMENTS:

- Apply chamomile, marigold or chickweed ointment to the areas two or three times a day.
- For red, inflamed skin, apply evening primrose oil with 1 or 2 drops lavender or rose essential oil. Or, apply aloe vera juice and a little turmeric.
- Support your immune and nervous systems by taking ½ tsp ashwagandha powder in warm rice or in oat milk, morning and evening; and taking a 500mg supplement of evening primrose oil.

021 BLEEDING GUMS

If your gums bleed, or if they are sore, red and inflamed, you have a form of gum disease that afflicts about three-quarters of the population over the age of 20. The early form of gum disease is known as gingivitis. At this stage careful brushing, flossing and regular cleaning by your hygienist can reverse any damage to your teeth or gums. However, left untreated gingivitis can progress to the point at which you may lose teeth. There is often a link between gum disease, adult-onset diabetes and a deficiency in vitamin C.

USEFUL HERBS: Echinacea (p.33), Sage (p.55), Marigold (p.26), Thyme (p.61), Rosemary (p.54), Hawthorn (p.31), Bilberry (p.65), Marsh mallow (p.23), Eyebright (p.35), Vervain (p.66), Nettle (p.64)

TREATMENTS:

- Make a mouthwash by adding 1 tsp of a mixture of equal parts echinacea, sage, marigold and thyme tinctures to a little warm water. Rinse the mouth for five minutes twice daily, after flossing.
- Dab any of the above tinctures or the tinctures of rosemary, hawthorn or bilberry directly onto sore or swollen gums.
- Fight the gum bacteria by taking ½ tsp echinacea tincture three times a day.
- Hawthorn and bilberry can help to strengthen gum tissue. Mix the powders with a little water to make a paste. Apply it directly to the gums.

022 HEAD LICE

Anyone with school-age children knows that head lice are becoming an epidemic, particularly as they are fast becoming immune to known treatments. The female louse attaches herself to the hair using claws and lays her eggs – at a rate of approximately eight eggs a day. The eggs themselves stick to the hair and are visible as little white specks. It is the eggs, rather than the lice, that we call nits. After eight days the eggs hatch and each louse lives for a further five weeks or so, piercing the skin on the scalp several times a day when hungry to feed on our blood. The bites look like little pinpricks and produce inflammation in the skin of the scalp. They also cause the itching that is so characteristic of head lice. The lice move from one child to another by close contact (they crawl from head to head, they do not jump or fly), especially from long hair that has been left loose, and they can live for 24 hours away from the body. If you are checking your child for head lice, you will find them most easily at the back of the head, hiding in among the hair.

Apart from the herbal treatments below, one of the best natural remedies is neem shampoo. Native to India, the neem tree produces seeds rich in chemical compounds that suppress the appetite in head lice, killing them off, and that prevent the unhatched eggs from developing. As the process is completely organic, the lice will not develop resistance to the treatment. Every night until the problem has gone, apply and rinse off the shampoo, then comb conditioner through the hair using a fine-tooth comb (or ideally a dedicated nit-comb) to remove the lice and eggs. You can dip the comb in hot cider vinegar to loosen the eggs from its teeth. To prevent the problem recurring, you should check all members of the family for lice. Do not share

towels or bed linen, and wash all potentially infected linen on a hot wash, which will kill both the lice and nits. If you have a tumble dryer, a hot dry cycle can provide an extra precaution, but is not essential. Boil all hair combs and brushes in water for ten to 15 minutes, to prevent reinfection.

USEFUL HERBS: Lavender (p.42), Rosemary (p.54), Peppermint (p.46), Basil (p.47), Cinnamon (p.29)

TREATMENTS:

- To remove both eggs and lice, mix 2 drops of the essential oil of basil, rosemary, peppermint or lavender in a base of 1 tsp olive oil and rub it into the scalp and hair at night. Leave the oil on the hair until the morning, and then wash it out thoroughly. (Put a towel over your pillow to prevent it becoming stained with the oil as you sleep.)

- Mix together 100ml (3½ fl. oz) olive oil, 20 drops basil oil and 30 drops tea tree oil. Apply the mixture to the hair in the evening and comb out the lice with a nit comb. Wash the hair the following morning. Repeat the process for five consecutive days. If necessary apply the mixture again in five days' time and repeat the cycle of applying, combing and washing for a further five days.

THE SKIN AND EYES

023 EYE STRAIN AND TIRED EYES

For those of us who spend long hours working at a computer screen or under strip lighting in air-conditioned offices, eyestrain is a common problem. Long periods of "close" work, such as reading or writing, can also cause tired, sore eyes. Try to make a conscious effort to look up and away every now and then. Pick a point in the distance and let your eyes gently rest there for a few minutes, without straining. Another good trick is to close your eyes and lightly place the palms of your hands over them. Leave your hands like this for a minute or two, then remove them and open your eyes. Eat antioxidant-rich foods, such as berries and kidney beans, to help protect your eyes from the effects of pollution. If your condition becomes chronic, consult your optician.

USEFUL HERBS: Rose (p.53), Chamomile (p.44), Fennel (p.37), Elder (p.56), Marigold (p.26), Plantain (p.52), Eyebright (p.35), Marsh mallow (p.23), Meadowsweet (p.36), Aloe vera (p.22), Bilberry (p.65)

TREATMENTS:

- Use cooling, soothing rose water to bathe your eyes at the end of the day.
- Lie down for ten to 15 minutes with a warm chamomile, fennel or elderflower teabag over each eye.
- Bathe your eyes with warm decoctions of marigold, plantain, eyebright or marsh mallow, all of which are soothing to the eyes.
- Take a daily supplement of bilberry.

024 STYES

When the glands at the base of the eyelashes become inflamed or infected, we develop a stye. Styes tend to develop when we are tired and run-down. Lasting about four or five days, the stye will feel sore and swollen, and eventually come to a head and then burst. Try not to rub your eye, as styes are contagious; and keep your towel and washcloth separate from those of other members of your household.

USEFUL HERBS: Eyebright (p.35), Marigold (p.26), Burdock (p.24), Echinacea (p.33), Rose (p.53), Elder (p.56), Marsh mallow (p.23), Chamomile (p.44), Plantain (p.52), Cleavers (p.38), Licorice (p.39), Red clover (p.63), Aloe vera (p.22)

TREATMENTS:

- Apply a warm compress for a few minutes every two to three hours to soothe the discomfort and help bring the stye to a head. Use an infusion or decoction of eyebright, chamomile, elderflower, marsh mallow, burdock, plantain or marigold.
- Alternatively, make the compress using 5 drops of one of the above herbs in tincture form and diluted in ½ cup distilled water, mixed with equal amounts of rose water.
- To detoxify your system and increase resistance to infection, take teas of burdock, echinacea, eyebright, rose, cleavers, licorice and red clover, individually or combined, three times daily.

025 CONJUNCTIVITIS

Conjunctivitis is an inflammatory eye condition, usually caused by infection, allergy (such as hay fever), or pollution. The whites of the eyes become red, and feel sore and irritated. The condition may make your eyes feel sensitive to light, and they may become weepy. On waking you will probably have a yellow crust at the corners of your eyes. If you suffer repeated bouts of conjunctivitis see your doctor in case something in your diet, often dairy products or the fungus candida, are at the root of the problem.

USEFUL HERBS: Eyebright (p.35), Elder (p.56), Chamomile (p.44), Marigold (p.26), Rose (p.53), Burdock (p.24), Nettle (p.64), Coriander (p.30), Fennel (p.37), Licorice (p.39), Aloe vera (p.22), Limeflower (p.62)

TREATMENTS:

• Eyebright is the best remedy for eye complaints. Bathe your eyes several times a day with cooled eyebright decoction.

• As an alternative to eyebright, make an eye-bath solution containing cooled elderflower, chamomile, or marigold decoction, or rose water.

• To clear inflammation and redness quickly, lie down for ten to 15 minutes with a lukewarm chamomile tea bag over each eye.

• To clear heat and inflammation, take teas or standard-dose tinctures of rose, nettle, burdock, eyebright or marigold, three times a day.

026 MUSCLE PAIN

If you have ever participated in a untypical bout of exercise, you will know about stiff muscles. However, severe muscle pain is usually brought on by cramp, muscle strain, or injuries such as a compressed nerve. This pain causes the affected and surrounding muscles to go into spasm – the body's safety mechanism to stop us doing further damage, but in itself intensely painful. Body-wide muscle pain may be a symptom of chronic stress, tiredness, or ME/post-viral syndrome.

USEFUL HERBS: Rosemary (p.54), Chamomile (p.44), Lavender (p.42), Basil (p.47), Thyme (p.61), Black cohosh (p.28), Ashwagandha (p.68), Ginger (p.69), Wild yam (p.32), Skullcap (p.57), Hawthorn (p.31), Sage (p.55), Cinnamon (p.29), Boneset (p.34), Hops (p.40), Peppermint (p.46), Passionflower (p.50), Parsley (p.51)

TREATMENTS:

• To ease tension and reduce spasm, gently massage the affected muscles using 2 drops rosemary, thyme, basil, lavender, chamomile or ginger essential oil in 1 tsp sesame oil.

• Add a few drops of a combination of the above oils to hot water. Soak a piece of gauze or cotton in the mixture and apply it as a hot compress to the affected muscle.

• Three times a day take teas or standard-dose tinctures of antispasmodic herbs, such as thyme, chamomile, ginger, basil, black cohosh, wild yam, and especially ashwagandha.

THE MUSCULO-SKELETAL SYSTEM

027 SCIATICA

The largest nerve in the body is called the sciatic nerve. It runs from the lower back, through the buttocks and down the back of the thigh. When the fibres of the sciatic nerve become inflamed, or when a vertebra places pressure on it owing to a misalignment of the spine or pelvis, we may feel pain down the whole nerve, all the way to the heel. This pain is known as sciatica. Congestion in the gut is a common underlying cause of sciatica, so avoid constipation by eating a healthy diet rich in fibre and fresh fruit and vegetables. Drink plenty of water to keep your kidneys working well. Always consult your doctor, or an osteopath or chiropracter about sciatica.

USEFUL HERBS: Lavender (p.42), Skullcap (p.57), Nettle (p.64), Meadowsweet (p.36), Ginger (p.69), Chamomile (p.44), Passionflower (p.50), Rosemary (p.54), Black cohosh (p.28), Vervain (p.66), Echinacea (p.33), Hops (p.40)

TREATMENTS:

• If you are feeling brave, sting yourself with some nettles at the area of pain. Chemicals in nettles trigger our anti-inflammatory response.

• For pain relief take a tea or standard-dose tincture of meadowsweet and echinacea, three times a day.

• To reduce pain and inflammation, massage the area with a little ginger grated into a blend of sesame oil and lemon juice.

• Apply a hot compress to the area using a tea of ginger or chamomile, as often as possible.

028 ARTHRITIS

There are many kinds of arthritis – rheumatoid arthritis (see right) and osteoarthritis, in which the cartilage between the joints begins to degenerate, causing stiffness and pain, are the most common. Diet is crucial in the treatment of arthritis. Avoid dairy produce, caffeine, vinegar, citrus fruits and other acidic fruits and vegetables (including tomatoes), processed and refined foods, alcohol, and shellfish, all of which can exacerbate joint problems. Prevent the build-up of toxins in your bowel (toxins can worsen the condition) by eating plenty of fibre.

USEFUL HERBS: Black cohosh (p.28), Wild yam (p.32), Ashwagandha (p.68), Lavender (p.42), Peppermint (p.46), Rosemary (p.54), Ginger (p.69), Burdock (p.24), Meadowsweet (p.36), Licorice (p.39), Aloe vera (p.22), Evening primrose (p.48), Cinnamon (p.29), Coriander (p.30), Echinacea (p.33), Cleavers (p.38), Parsley (p.51), Elder (p.56), Skullcap (p.57), Chickweed (p.59), Dandelion (p.60), Thyme (p.61), Limeflower (p.62), Bilberry (p.65)

TREATMENTS:

• Ashwagandha is both anti-inflammatory and painkilling. Take it as a milk decoction, twice daily.

• To reduce inflammation and clear toxins, take burdock, meadowsweet and nettle in teas or standard-dose tinctures three times a day.

• Ease stiff joints by rubbing them with oils of peppermint, rosemary or lavender diluted in 1 tsp sesame oil.

029 RHEUMATISM

Inflammatory disorders of the muscles, stiff joints, and various types of arthritis are all forms of rheumatism, and they all cause pain. Rheumatism is brought on, or exacerbated, by such things as stress, constipation (causing a state of toxicity in the body), poor digestion and absorption, and deficiencies of certain nutrients (from a diet low in fresh fruit and vegetables, and essential fatty acids). Try to cut out red meat from your diet, and avoid tomatoes, citrus fruits, cheese, caffeine and alcohol, all of which can aggravate the condition.

USEFUL HERBS: Black cohosh (p.28), Boneset (p.34), Burdock (p.24), Fennel (p.37), Nettle (p.64), Wild yam (p.32), Yarrow (p.20), Meadowsweet (p.36), Licorice (p.39), Ashwagandha (p.68), Ginger (p.69), Peppermint (p.46), Rosemary (p.54), Dandelion (p.60), Cinnamon (p.29), Elecampane (p.41), Evening primrose (p.48), Parsley (p.51), Chickweed (p.59), Bilberry (p.65)

TREATMENTS:
- Meadowsweet, black cohosh, licorice and wild yam are anti-inflammatory. Take them as teas or standard-dose tinctures, three times daily.
- Take teas of fennel, nettle, boneset, yarrow, meadowsweet and burdock, which cleanse toxins from the blood stream, three times daily.
- Rub painkilling and anti-inflammatory oils into painful muscles and joints. Use a base of 1 tsp ashwagandha or sesame oil and add 2 drops ginger, peppermint or rosemary oil.

030 OSTEOPOROSIS

Osteoporosis may be the result of a calcium deficiency; or it may be related to falling levels of estrogen, the female sex hormone that plays a part in the ongoing regeneration of bone, during the menopause. The disease is often associated with ageing (as we get older the body finds it harder to absorb calcium from our food). If a woman has been a lifelong dieter, or has taken little exercise or had a total hysterectomy, or if you suffer from coeliac disease or diabetes, or you smoke, you may be at a higher risk of developing osteoporosis. Symptoms include low-back pain, height loss, stooped posture, and frequent fractures.

USEFUL HERBS: Wild yam (p.32), Black cohosh (p.28), Marigold (p.26), Dandelion (p.60), Ginseng (p.49), Hops (p.40), Licorice (p.39), Nettle (p.64), Sage (p.55), Plantain (p.52), Thyme (p.61), Wild oats (p.25), Elecampane (p.41), Peppermint (p.46), Boneset (p.34)

TREATMENTS:
- Wild yam, black cohosh, hops, marigold, sage, licorice and ginseng contain plant estrogens. Take them in teas or as standard-dose tinctures three times a day.
- Take calcium-rich herbs, including nettles, plantain, wild oats, thyme, licorice, elecampane, peppermint and boneset, regularly as part of your diet, or in teas.
- Dandelion leaves contain calcium and boron, which protects the bones from calcium-loss. Add them regularly to salads and teas.

THE MUSCULO-SKELETAL SYSTEM

THE MUSCULO-SKELETAL SYSTEM

031 BURSITIS AND TENDONITIS

Bursitis and tendonitis (or repetitive strain injury) are caused by over-use of the joints. Tendonitis is an inflammation of the tendons, the fibrous tissues that connect muscles to bones, and tends to occur in the wrists and shoulders. Bursitis is an inflammation of the bursae, the fluid-filled sacs that lubricate our joints in places where muscles and tendons meet bone, and tends to occur in the wrist joints. Both can be extremely painful and even incapacitating.

USEFUL HERBS: Meadowsweet (p.36), Black cohosh (p.28), Ginger (p.69), Echinacea (p.33), Licorice (p.39), Nettle (p.64), Lavender (p.42), Rosemary (p.54), Peppermint (p.46)

TREATMENTS:

- Take a cup of meadowsweet tea, or 1 tsp meadowsweet tincture, three or four times a day to manage the pain.
- Gotu cola increases blood supply to the area of pain and speeds tissue-healing. Take it in a tea or standard-dose tincture, three times daily.
- To ease inflammation try tea made with black cohosh three times a day.
- To ease pain massage the joints gently with 2 drops rosemary, lavender or peppermint oil, diluted in 1 tsp sesame oil.
- For connective-tissue injuries, such as tennis elbow, take, as a tea or standard-dose tincture, a mixture of echinacea, nettles, ginger and licorice, three times a day.

032 GOUT

Gout is a form of arthritis and causes pain in the joints, usually beginning with the big toe. The condition is caused by a build-up in the blood of uric acid, a biproduct of digestion, usually excreted in our urine. When the levels of uric acid become abnormally high, crystals form and collect in the joints causing pain, swelling and inflammation. Gout is associated with a diet high in fatty foods, red meat, and alcohol (particularly beer), and also high in tomatoes, cheese and citrus fruits. Among the best foods for combating gout are celery seeds, which help to clear uric acid – drink a cup of celery-seed tea every day. According to the Amazons avocado has the same effect.

USEFUL HERBS: Nettle (p.64), Meadowsweet (p.36), Echinacea (p.33), Burdock (p.24), Bilberry (p.65), Cleavers (p.38), Fennel (p.37), Parsley (p.51), Rosemary (p.54), Sage (p.55), Elder (p.56), Chickweed (p.59), Dandelion (p.60), Thyme (p.61), Limeflower (p.62)

TREATMENTS:

- Drink nettle tea, which is both detoxifying and diuretic and so will help to clear uric acid from the blood. Add nettles to soups, too.
- Drink meadowsweet tea; its salicylates help to relieve pain and inflammation.
- Take, as a tea or standard-dose tincture, a combination of burdock, meadowsweet and echinacea to clear uric acid. Add licorice and wild yam to reduce swelling, and take three times a day.

033 COLDS AND FLU

There are 200 or more different viruses that can cause the collection of symptoms that we call a cold. When we are run-down, tired, stressed, or suffering from poor absorption and elimination in the gut, a cold or flu virus can take hold. As the body begins the process of detoxification and recovery from the infection, we experience the symptoms of a cold – a heavy head, blocked or runny nose, and fever. Take supplements of vitamin C and zinc to keep colds at bay, or to speed your recovery.

USEFUL HERBS: Boneset (p.34), Elder (p.56), Peppermint (p.46), Yarrow (p.20), Ginger (p.69), Cinnamon (p.29), Coriander (p.30), Thyme (p.61), Lavender (p.42), Lemon balm (p.45), Garlic (p.21), Echinacea (p.33), Rosemary (p.54), Licorice (p.39)

TREATMENTS:

- As soon as the first symptoms of a cold or flu appear, take ½ tsp echinacea tincture, every two hours; and three times a day take ½ tsp of a mixture of equal parts grated ginger, licorice powder, black pepper and cardamom, stirred into 1 tsp runny honey.
- Take hot boneset tea every two hours at the first signs of the flu. Boneset relieves the aches and pains of flu, helps to throw off fevers, and clears congestion in the sinuses and throat.
- To help clear mucus and catarrh, make a steam inhalation using teas or oils of thyme, peppermint, lavender, cinnamon or rosemary.

034 CATARRH AND SINUSITIS

When the lining of the respiratory tract is irritated, it secretes more mucous, which builds up into catarrh. Sinusitis is the name given to the inflammation of the membranes in the sinuses. Both catarrh and sinusitis may occur in a chronic form, with or without infection (such as a cold), as a result of pollution, or as an attempt by the body to eliminate toxins. A milk allergy can also cause catarrh, as can a poor diet that has been overindulged in starches, sugar and salt, and is lacking in essential vitamins and minerals.

USEFUL HERBS: Chamomile (p.44), Peppermint (p.46), Marigold (p.26), Ginger (p.69), Cinnamon (p.29), Garlic (p.21), Yarrow (p.20), Eyebright (p.35), Elder (p.56), Plantain (p.52), Rose (p.53), Marsh mallow (p.23), Coriander (p.30)

TREATMENTS:

- To clear congestion drink a hot tea of grated, fresh ginger root, three to six times a day; and three times a day take ½ or 1 tsp coriander or cinnamon in 1 tsp runny honey (you can also take these spices as decoctions).
- Take teas or standard-dose tinctures of marsh mallow and plantain, or aloe vera juice, to cool inflammation in the sinuses.
- Make an Inhalation using hot teas of thyme, elderflower, basil, chamomile or peppermint; or by placing a few drops of their essential oils in hot water. Drape a towel over your head and breathe in the steam to clear congestion.

THE RESPIRATORY SYSTEM

THE RESPIRATORY SYSTEM

035 TINNITUS

Tinnitus is a ringing, roaring, buzzing, humming or hissing in the ears, and is often associated with ageing. Although in most cases it is hard for doctors to pinpoint the precise cause of tinnitus, catarrhal congestion, stress, wax, nutritional deficiencies (such as a lack of zinc), taking diuretics or other drugs (such as aspirin), and anemia have known links. Consistent exposure to loud noises, such as machinery or gunfire, or having the volume too high on a personal stereo, may also cause tinnitus. Spinal or muscle problems in the neck may also be triggers, so it can be helpful to consult a chiropractor or osteopath.

USEFUL HERBS: Black cohosh (p.28), Skullcap (p.57), Hops (p.40), Passionflower (p.50), Hawthorn (p.31), Garlic (p.21), Gotu cola (p.27), Vervain (p.66), Chamomile (p.44), Lavender (p.42), Ashwagandha (p.68)

TREATMENTS:

- Take hawthorn and black cohosh, individually or combined in teas or standard-dose tinctures, three times a day for several months.
- To ease any contributory stress and tension take skullcap, ashwagandha, chamomile, vervain or gotu cola as teas or standard-dose tinctures.
- Massage the neck with 1 tsp warm ashwagandha or sesame oil, combined with 2 drops lavender, chamomile or rosemary oil.
- To improve circulation to the ear, take a clove of garlic, or two capsules, twice daily.

036 EARACHE

The ears, nose and throat are closely connected and earache is often caused by pains in the throat, and in the nasal passages and mouth, as well as from a bacterial infection in the middle ear or inflammation in the outer ear. If you suspect you or your child has a middle-ear infection consult your doctor. If you suffer from frequent ear infections, you may have underlying problems with your throat or sinuses, or they may be associated with chronic catarrh.

USEFUL HERBS: Lavender (p.42), Garlic (p.21), Chamomile (p.44), Skullcap (p.57), Echinacea (p.33), Licorice (p.39), Elder (p.56), Cleavers (p.38), Rose (p.53), Hops (p.40), Black cohosh (p.28), Thyme (p.61), Lemon balm (p.45), Passionflower (p.50)

TREATMENTS:

- To ease the pain take teas or standard-dose tinctures of hops, chamomile, passionflower, black cohosh or skullcap every two hours.
- As long as you do not have a perforated eardrum, make pain-relieving eardrops using 1 tsp sesame or olive oil combined with 2 drops of either lavender, chamomile, thyme, lemon balm or rose oil. Warm the mixture and place 2 or 3 drops in each ear. You can also use this mixture for a gentle massage around the ears and throat, or in hot water as an inhalation.
- Take ¼–½ tsp echinacea tincture every two hours to help resolve the infection.

037 TONSILLITIS

The tonsils are two small, round lymph glands that lie either side of the throat. When they become inflamed, as a result of bacterial or viral infection, the condition is known as tonsillitis, and frequently occurs in children, especially those under nine. (As we get older the tonsils tend to become smaller and less prone to infection.) The tonsils produce antibodies that help to kill microorganisms that might cause infection in our respiratory or digestive tract.

Acute tonsillitis can be caused by an infection from a virus or from streptococcal bacteria. The illness causes pus-filled spots to develop on the inflamed tonsils, as well as a fever, pain and difficulty in swallowing, and a sore throat. Chronic or recurrent tonsillitis can persist for months and is related to lowered immunity, allergies (such as milk allergy), and an overburdened lymphatic system (usually as a result of the body being overloaded with toxins). Always consult a doctor if your child has a fever with tonsillitis, to rule out streptococcal infection (which if left untreated can affect the heart or kidneys).

USEFUL HERBS: Sage (p.55), Thyme (p.61), Chamomile (p.44), Marsh mallow (p.23), Burdock (p.24), Echinacea (p.33), Lavender (p.42), Rose (p.53), Cleavers (p.38), Marigold (p.26), Meadowsweet (p.36), Black cohosh (p.28), Lemon balm (p.45), Coriander (p.30)

TREATMENTS: For acute tonsillitis
- Take ¼–½ tsp echinacea tincture every two hours to help resolve the infection.
- Take teas or standard-dose tinctures, three to six times a day, of herbs specifically indicated for the tonsils: cleavers, marigold and burdock.
- Gargle or make throat sprays using antiseptic herbs, such as chamomile, rose, sage or thyme. Neat lemon juice will do the trick too.
- Apply to the throat hot compresses made using chamomile or burdock tea.
- Massage the throat area using the essential oils of lavender, chamomile, thyme, rosemary, rose or lemon balm (at a ratio of 2 drops essential oil diluted in a base of 1 tsp sesame oil).
- During infection drink cups of coriander tea throughout the day.
- To soothe pain on swallowing, take teas of marsh mallow, meadowsweet, black cohosh and licorice throughout the day.

TREATMENTS: For chronic or recurrent tonsillitis
- Take ½ tsp echinacea tincture three times daily to help boost the immune system.
- Use gargles or throat sprays of sage and thyme, or rose and chamomile, three times a day.
- Massage the diluted oils (2 drops per teaspoon of base oil) of lavender, rose or chamomile into the throat, night and morning.
- Take teas or standard-dose tinctures of cleavers, marigold and/or burdock to help the tonsils in their cleansing work until the problem resolves.

THE RESPIRATORY SYSTEM

THE RESPIRATORY SYSTEM

038 SORE THROAT

A sore throat usually heralds the onset of a cold or the flu. However, anything that dries up the normally moist and smooth mucous membranes of the respiratory tract can cause a sore throat – including tobacco smoke, allergies, dry heat and too much shouting. If a child has an acute sore throat accompanied by a fever and swollen tonsils, consult your doctor as a streptococcal infection can have serious consequences.

USEFUL HERBS: Echinacea (p.33), Garlic (p.21), Sage (p.55), Elder (p.56), Thyme (p.61), Rosemary (p.54), Cleavers (p.38), Marsh mallow (p.23), Marigold (p.26), Licorice (p.39), Boneset (p.34), Coriander (p.30), Eyebright (p.35), Chickweed (p.59), Bilberry (p.65)

TREATMENTS:

• Take ¼–½ tsp echinacea tincture every two hours to help fight the infection.

• Sip marsh mallow and licorice tea throughout the day to soothe the discomfort in the throat.

• Place ½ tsp of a mixture of sage and thyme tincture in a little water and use it as an antiseptic gargle or throat spray, three times a day. (Neat lemon juice makes a good antiseptic throat spray, too.)

• If your sore throat is a herald to a cold or the flu, drink regular cups of boneset and elderflower tea. This will help to throw off any aches and pains, and bring down a fever.

039 SWOLLEN GLANDS

When we talk of swollen glands, we usually mean the lymph nodes that lie in our neck, groin or armpit. Part of the lymphatic system and essential to our immunity, the lymph nodes have two functions. First they filter the lymph fluid, which carries the nutrients of digested food into the blood stream and deports waste products, including foreign microorganisms and toxins, away from it. Second they store infection-fighting white blood cells (lymphocytes). As they filter the lymph, the nodes trap the waste, toxins and microorganisms and release lymphocytes to fight any potential infection. When the lymph nodes become overloaded with toxins, or have to fight hard to see off a general or local infection (and sometimes cancer), they swell.

USEFUL HERBS: Cleavers (p.38), Echinacea (p.33), Licorice (p.39), Red clover (p.63), Marigold (p.26), Dandelion (p.60), Burdock (p.24), Gotu cola (p.27), Ashwagandha (p.68)

TREATMENTS:

• Take cleavers tea three times a day. This is a specific remedy to help reduce enlarged lymph nodes. Cleavers also helps the lymphatic system in its detoxifying work.

• To aid detoxification take, as teas or standard-dose tinctures, red clover, gotu cola, marigold, burdock and dandelion root three times daily.

• Take ½ tsp ashwagandha and licorice, mixed with honey and a little water, three times a day, to help support your body's immune system.

040 LARYNGITIS

Laryngitis is the inflammation and infection of the larynx, otherwise known as the vocal chords, and causes a sore throat, pain when you talk, and a hoarse voice. The condition can develop from an infection in the mouth, nose or throat, from mucus dripping down the throat during a cold, with tonsillitis or bronchitis, as a result of irritation from a smoky atmosphere, or from too much singing, talking or shouting. If you suffer from chronic laryngitis, consult a doctor.

USEFUL HERBS: Sage (p.55), Thyme (p.61), Echinacea (p.33), Licorice (p.39), Elder (p.56), Black cohosh (p.28), Lavender (p.42), Garlic (p.21), Marsh mallow (p.23), Plantain (p.52), Chamomile (p.44), Rosemary (p.54)

TREATMENTS:

• Take ¼–½ tsp echinacea tincture in a little water every two hours, to help fight infection.

• To ease discomfort in your larynx, take soothing teas of marsh mallow, licorice and plantain, three to six times a day.

• If you have a tight, croupy cough, take teas or standard-dose tinctures of thyme, chamomile and black cohosh, three times a day.

• To ease pain and spasm in your larynx, make a double-strength infusion of lavender, rosemary, thyme, chamomile or basil and pour it into a bowl. Use this as a steam inhalation.

• Massage your throat with 2 drops basil or lavender oil in a base of 1 tsp warm sesame oil.

041 ASTHMA

An asthma attack narrows the airways in the lungs, which can then become inflamed and filled with mucus. The more the airways become blocked, the more difficult it is to breathe. There are many triggers for asthma – including rising levels of pollution. However, among other things, certain foods (particularly milk products), dust mites, emotional upsets, or a digestive or respiratory infection can also trigger asthma. To help prevent asthma combine changes in diet with herbal remedies – which you may need to take over several months to make lasting improvement. See a doctor if you have an attack.

USEFUL HERBS: Marsh mallow (p.23), Black cohosh (p.28), Elecampane (p.41), Thyme (p.61), Ashwagandha (p.68), Ginger (p.69), Licorice (p.39), Chamomile (p.44), Garlic (p.21), Lavender (p.42), Lemon balm (p.45), Evening primrose (p.48), Passionflower (p.50), Rosemary (p.54), Elder (p.56), Chickweed (p.59), Nettle (p.64)

TREATMENTS:

• Take regular doses of raw garlic (or garlic capsules), which will help to clear mucus from the chest and ease coughing and wheezing.

• Take teas or standard-dose tinctures of the expectorants elecampane, thyme and licorice, individually or in a combination of your choice.

• If you suffer from acute asthma, try a tea made using equal parts chamomile, thyme and elecampane, with ½ part black cohosh. Drink it every hour or so.

THE RESPIRATORY SYSTEM

042 HAY FEVER

During the late spring and summer, as the weather gets warmer, high numbers of grass pollens are released into the air. In people susceptible to hay fever (which is also known as allergic rhinitis), the pollen stimulates the body's production of histamine, a compound released by our cells in response to an allergic reaction (among other things). The histamine dilates the capillaries, contracts the body's smooth tissue, and irritates the mucus-secreting glands. The results are all the symptoms of hay fever, including an itching, running nose; red, streaming, irritated eyes; a blocked nose; a tickly throat; a sensitive palate; and itchy skin. Hay fever symptoms tend to be at their worst first thing in the morning and last thing in the evening. Dust mites and animal dander can also produce hay fever-like symptoms. People who suffer from asthma or eczema are especially prone to hay fever (and conversely some studies suggest that around one third of hay-fever sufferers may develop asthma).

There are many herbal treatments to help ease hay-fever symptoms, and several pieces of dietary advice. For example, local honey contains the pollens that trigger your hay fever, because the local bees have used these pollens to make their honey. Acclimatize your immune system to the allergens by taking 1 or 2 dessertspoonful of regional honey with each meal for between two and four months before the season begins. Also, once the hay fever season is under way, omit wheat from your diet as it can exacerbate allergic reactions in some people; and if your hay fever is chronic, omit dairy produce, too. Dairy foods encourage the production of mucus in the body; while in some people hay fever is associated with a milk allergy.

USEFUL HERBS: Eyebright (p.35), Echinacea (p.33), Chamomile (p.44), Elder (p.56), Licorice (p.39), Yarrow (p.20), Lemon balm (p.45), Plantain (p.52), Nettle (p.64), Rose (p.53), Ashwagandha (p.68)

TREATMENTS:

• As a preventative measure, between two and four months before the hay-fever season begins, take ginseng, nettle and echinacea twice daily to boost your immune system.

• Three to six times a day take herbs that will help to reduce allergic tendencies. Take teas or standard-dose tinctures of elderflower, echinacea, chamomile, licorice, lemon balm and yarrow, individually or in combination.

• Take teas of plantain and eyebright, three times daily, to tone the mucus membranes of the nasal passages, helping to desensitize them to allergens and to clear catarrhal congestion.

• Take regular infusions of nettles. Nettle reduces the inflammation of the mucus membranes and, taken consistently over time, will make you less sensitive to the effects of pollen.

• If you have streaming eyes, bathe them using a wash of rose water; or with 2 drops chamomile tincture diluted in 2 cups cooled, boiled water.

043 COUGHS

A cough is nature's way of keeping the airways clear so that we can breathe freely. It is a reflex response to remove anything blocking the throat or bronchial tubes. This is most often catarrh, but could be something irritating that you have inhaled, such as dust. Smoking and infection are the most common causes of coughs. A cough often begins by being dry and irritating. As mucus production increases, in an attempt to protect the lining of the chest, the cough loosens and becomes more productive.

USEFUL HERBS: Marsh mallow (p.23), Licorice (p.39), Echinacea (p.33), Thyme (p.61), Garlic (p.21), Elecampane (p.41), Cinnamon (p.29), Ginger (p.69), Rosemary (p.54), Basil (p.47), Lemon balm (p.45), Coriander (p.30), Hops (p.40), Linseed (p.43), Red clover (p.63)

TREATMENTS:
- Make a hot, herbal inhalation using the teas of the decongestant, anti-inflammatory and expectorant herbs thyme, rose and licorice. Pour into a bowl and breathe in the steam.
- For a cough brought on by a chest infection, take garlic raw or in capsules and ½ tsp echinacea tincture, with teas or standard-dose tinctures of elecampane, thyme and licorice, three times a day.
- For a dry, irritating cough, take soothing marsh mallow, plantain and licorice, as a tea or standard-dose tincture, three to six times a day.

044 BRONCHITIS

Bronchitis occurs when the bronchial tubes in the lungs become inflamed as a result of smoking, pollution, or viral or bacterial infection. Chronic bronchitis is a result of repeated attacks of acute bronchitis. The aim of any treatment is to get the mucus out of your lungs and respiratory tubes. Mucus-filled lungs not only cause difficulty in breathing, but also breed bacteria, which can cause pneumonia.

USEFUL HERBS: Licorice (p.39), Thyme (p.61), Elecampane (p.41), Elder (p.56), Garlic (p.21), Ginger (p.69), Rose (p.53), Marsh mallow (p.23), Ashwagandha (p.68), Plantain (p.52), Lavender (p.42), Cinnamon (p.29), Lemon balm (p.45), Chamomile (p.44), Rosemary (p.54), Boneset (p.34), Fennel (p.37), Linseed (p.43), Red clover (p.63)

TREATMENTS:
- Take teas or standard-dose tinctures of thyme, elecampane and licorice every two hours in acute infections and three times a day for chronic problems.
- If the cough is dry and irritating take teas or standard-dose tinctures of marsh mallow, licorice, plantain, thyme and elecampane; if it is more productive use thyme, ginger, basil, rose and lavender. (Frequency as above.)
- Breathe in the steam from a bowl of hot ginger and thyme tea, or from a few drops of the oils of rose, thyme, ginger, cinnamon, lemon balm, chamomile or rosemary in hot water.

THE RESPIRATORY SYSTEM

THE CIRCULATORY SYSTEM

045 COLD HANDS AND FEET

If your circulation is poor, perhaps through stress or tension or a lack of exercise, the blood supply to your extremities will be slow and you will tend to feel the cold, particularly in your hands and feet. You may look pale and be prone to chilblains, lethargy, sluggish digestion, and constipation. Avoid caffeine and try to stop smoking, which both constrict the blood vessels and aggravate tension. Eat plenty of essential fatty acids, such as those found in oily fish, and foods rich in vitamin C and bioflavonoids (such as citrus fruits), which will all improve circulation. Exercise regularly.

USEFUL HERBS: Garlic (p.21), Ginger (p.69), Cinnamon (p.29), Peppermint (p.46), Yarrow (p.20), Elder (p.56), Coriander (p.30), Hawthorn (p.31), Thyme (p.61), Rosemary (p.54), Basil (p.47), Limeflower (p.62), Wild yam (p.32), Echinacea (p.33), Boneset (p.34)

TREATMENTS:

- Begin the day with a hot cup of ginger tea made by infusing freshly grated ginger in hot water. Hand and foot baths of strong ginger tea can also warm you from head to toe.
- Use warming spices regularly in your cooking: ginger, coriander seeds, and cinnamon will all stimulate the circulation.
- Alternate teas made with warming spices with teas using herbs that bring blood to the surface of the body: lemon balm, basil, thyme, elderflower, peppermint, limeflower and yarrow.

046 CHILBLAINS

If you suffer from poor circulation to your hands and feet, you may well be prone to chilblains. These red or purple shiny lumps develop because the circulation is not supplying the fingers and toes with enough oxygen and nutrients (in the blood) to keep the tissues healthy. Chilblains can be painful, inflamed and itchy, and are often exacerbated by stress, poor diet, lack of exercise, or the onset of an infection. Raynaud's syndrome (poor blood-flow to the hands causing them to go blue or even white) and heart or arterial problems can also cause chilblains. As well as the remedies below, any of the remedies for poor circulation (see cold hands and feet, left) will help to prevent chilblains.

USEFUL HERBS: Ginger (p.69), Marigold (p.26), Cinnamon (p.29), Lavender (p.42), Thyme (p.61), Rosemary (p.54), Hawthorn (p.31), Peppermint (p.46), Yarrow (p.20), Elder (p.56), Coriander (p.30), Garlic (p.21)

TREATMENTS:

- If your chilblains are unbroken, soak them in strong ginger tea for ten to 15 minutes once or twice a day to stimulate the circulation.
- Relieve itching chilblains by rubbing into them either marigold ointment or oil of lavender.
- To stimulate the circulation and soothe your chilblains, take hot foot baths using strong teas of ginger, cinnamon, thyme or rosemary; or make the foot baths using a few drops of these herbs' essential oils in hot water.

047 PALPITATIONS

Heart palpitations occur when the heart misses a beat or two, or, more commonly, beats rapidly for a short time. The cause of palpitations is a surge of adrenaline, which is perfectly normal after physical exercise, but is abnormal during periods of stress, nervousness, or emotional upset; with hot flushes during the menopause; and after drinking excessive amounts of caffeine. Palpitations can be minor and self-limiting, but to be safe, always refer heart irregularities to a doctor, and check your treatments with him or her.

USEFUL HERBS: Skullcap (p.57), Hawthorn (p.31), Chamomile (p.44), Lavender (p.42), Hops (p.40), Passionflower (p.50), Limeflower (p.62), Rosemary (p.54), Lemon balm (p.45), Vervain (p.66), Black cohosh (p.28), Wild yam (p.32)

TREATMENTS:

- Hawthorn is the best tonic for the heart, regulating heartbeat, strengthening the heart muscle, and improving blood-flow through the heart. Take a tea or standard-dose tincture two or three times a day.
- For stress-related palpitations, calm the heart by taking any of the following relaxing herbs with hawthorn as a tea or standard-dose tincture: hops, passionflower, lemon balm, chamomile, vervain, lavender or skullcap.
- Limeflower tea relaxes the coronary arteries, easing palpitations. Combine it with hawthorn.

048 CRAMP

When a muscle goes into spasm we experience cramp. Muscle spasms can be a result of low calcium levels and certain vitamin deficiencies, particularly vitamins B or D. Optimize your diet by eating plenty of fresh fruit and vegetables that are rich in all the vitamins and minerals your body needs. Take supplements of vitamin C to aid circulation. Warming spices, such as cinnamon, coriander and turmeric will help your circulation, too. Eat plenty of fibre and take lots of exercise to optimize your digestion and maximize the blood-flow throughout the body.

USEFUL HERBS: Hawthorn (p.31), Garlic (p.21), Ginger (p.69), Rosemary (p.54), Cinnamon (p.29), Parsley (p.51), Limeflower (p.62), Peppermint (p.46), Elder (p.56), Basil (p.47), Yarrow (p.20), Coriander (p.30), Nettle (p.64), Thyme (p.61), Wild oats (p.25), Lemon balm (p.45), Black cohosh (p.28)

TREATMENTS:

- Massage the affected area vigorously with 2 drops of the essential oils of cinnamon, coriander, ginger or rosemary, diluted in a base of 1 tsp sesame oil.
- Increase your intake of calcium by adding nettles, thyme, parsley and wild oats to your diet. You can also drink them regularly as teas.
- Take regular cups of hot tea made with circulation-stimulating herbs, such as yarrow, limeflower, basil, rosemary, elderflower, peppermint, thyme and lemon balm.

THE CIRCULATORY SYSTEM

THE CIRCULATORY SYSTEM

049 BLOOD-PRESSURE PROBLEMS

Our blood reaches every part of our anatomy by travelling along a network of arteries. These arteries should be elastic enough to allow the blood to pulse along them at an even pressure, expanding and contracting as necessary. However, among other things, hardening of the arterial walls (for example, through poor diet, old age, or stress, or fatty deposits along the insides of the arteries, say as a result of obesity and smoking) can constrict the space through which the blood can flow and cause hypertension – high blood pressure. The long-term effects of high blood pressure can be serious. In particular it can weaken the heart, kidneys and liver. Staggeringly, around one third of adults in the West suffer from high blood pressure. As a means to combat hypertension, eat a diet rich with blood-pressure-regulating nutrients such as calcium, magnesium and potassium. Foods such as oily fish, olive oil, nuts, seeds, beans, pulses, whole grains and garlic will all help with this. Also, try to eat less meat, particularly red meat. Avoid caffeine, alcohol and smoking, and exercise regularly. Always consult a doctor about hypertension.

Less common is hypotension – low blood pressure – which tends to occur in the elderly, when we are dehydrated or run-down from illness or stress, or during cold weather.

USEFUL HERBS: High blood pressure: Hawthorn (p.31), Limeflower (p.62), Garlic (p.21), Yarrow (p.20), Passionflower (p.50), Skullcap (p.57), Chamomile (p.44), Vervain (p.66), Evening primrose (p.48), Black cohosh (p.28); Low blood pressure: Ginger (p.69), Hawthorn (p.31), Cinnamon (p.29), Rosemary (p.54), Garlic (p.69)

TREATMENTS: For high blood pressure
- Hawthorn flowers, leaves and berries act as a tonic to the whole arterial system and will help to balance blood pressure. Take hawthorn as a tea or standard-dose tincture three times a day. (This herb is also good for low blood pressure.)
- Take a tea or standard-dose tincture of limeflower to dilate the arteries and dandelion leaves, which are diuretic, three times a day.
- To treat hypertension caused by stress, blend chamomile, passionflower or skullcap with hawthorn or limeflower in teas; or have a relaxing bath laced with a few drops of lavender or lemon balm oil.
- Eat plenty of raw garlic in your daily diet, or take it in capsules every day.

TREATMENTS: For low blood pressure
- Add ginger, cinnamon, garlic and other warming spices to your diet.
- Add a few drops of stimulating essential oils, such as rosemary, ginger and cinnamon to your bathwater.
- Massage your body using 2 drops rosemary oil diluted in 1 tsp sesame oil.

050 ATHEROSCLEROSIS

Atherosclerosis is a condition in which cholesterol-rich deposits, called plaque, cause narrowing in the space in the arteries. It limits the flow of blood to the muscle tissues, including the heart. The lack of oxygen and nourishment to the heart triggers anginal pain, and poses a major risk of heart attack. The condition can be aggravated by high blood pressure. The build-up of plaque in the artery walls, can be a result of eating too much animal fat and sugar, and of alcohol, smoking, lack of exercise, and obesity. Try to reduce your intake of fat, and try to make the fat that you do eat vegetable and polyunsaturated in origin (such as cold-pressed olive, sunflower, or soya oil).

USEFUL HERBS: Bilberry (p.65), Garlic (p.21), Ginger (p.69), Red clover (p.63), Meadowsweet (p.36), Hawthorn (p.31), Limeflower (p.62), Ginseng (p.49)

TREATMENTS:

- Eat ginger every day – its antioxidants protect the blood vessels against cholesterol damage.
- Eat raw garlic in your daily diet, or take capsules; garlic lowers cholesterol.
- Take bilberries as they will lower cholesterol, open the blood vessels, and help prevent clots.
- Take red clover or meadowsweet in a tea or standard-dose tincture three times every day. Red clover reduces cholesterol absorption; and meadowsweet contains salicylate salts, which soften the deposits of atherosclerosis.

051 RAISED CHOLESTEROL

Cholesterol is a waxy substance in the blood that both contributes to the build-up of plaque in the arteries and to heart disease. A quarter of the body's cholesterol comes from diet and three-quarters is made in the liver. The body uses the liver's cholesterol to make hormones and for nutrition. There are two types of cholesterol, low density lipoproteins (LDL), which increase the risk of heart attacks, and high density lipoproteins (HDL), which actually reduce it. Vitamin B3 (niacin) lowers LDL and raises HDL, so take B-vitamin supplements. Also, plant fibres can lower cholesterol. A diet high in fruit and vegetables (particularly avocados, celery, asparagus and carrots) and whole grains, coupled with only small amounts of fats, will help to keep your cholesterol levels normal. Finally, take regular aerobic exercise.

USEFUL HERBS: Garlic (p.21), Hawthorn (p.31), Ginger (p.69), Licorice (p.39), Red clover (p.63), Evening primrose (p.48), Wild oats (p.25)

TREATMENTS:

- Eat a clove of raw garlic every day; this can lower cholesterol levels by ten to 15 per cent.
- Take ginger, evening primrose and licorice as teas or standard-dose tinctures to lower cholesterol; add hawthorn to protect the arteries from damage caused by the build-up of plaque.
- Take red clover as a tea or standard-dose tincture three times a day. This herb is known to reduce the absorption of cholesterol.

THE CIRCULATORY SYSTEM

052 ANEMIA

Anemia – low numbers of red blood cells – can make you feel lethargic, agitated and unhappy, and when you exert yourself can cause headaches and dizziness. Poor diet, poor digestion, too much caffeine or alcohol, and too much fibre can all cause anemia because they all hamper the body's ability to absorb iron, which is essential for the production of red blood cells. However, blood loss as a result of bleeding gums, hemorrhoids, a peptic ulcer and heavy periods can also be to blame. To prevent and remedy anemia, ensure that your diet is rich in iron, folic acid, protein, and vitamins C, E and B12.

USEFUL HERBS: Parsley (p.51), Nettle (p.64), Dandelion (p.60), Chickweed (p.59), Coriander (p.30), Burdock (p.24), Vervain (p.66), Hawthorn (p.31), Bilberry (p.65), Hops (p.40), Ginger (p.69)

TREATMENTS:

• Parsley, dandelion leaves, nettle, and coriander leaves are all rich in iron and folic acid. Add them regularly to your salads and garnishes.

• To improve iron-absorption drink teas of iron-rich digestive herbs, such as burdock, vervain, hawthorn and hops; or a cup of fresh ginger tea before meals.

• Bilberries are rich in vitamin C, which enhances the absorption of iron. Eat ½ cup of the fresh berries every day, or drink a cup of bilberry decoction three times a day.

053 VARICOSE VEINS AND HEMORRHOIDS

Varicose veins most often occur in the legs. When the valves that push blood along the veins stop working, blood begins to stagnate and the vein expands and twists. In the anal region this problem is known as hemorrhoids. Either condition can cause discomfort, even pain, and hemorrhoids may itch or burn and they tend to bleed. Both are usually hereditary and are aggravated by too much standing or too little exercise, or pregnancy, constipation, obesity, shallow breathing, and stress. Supplements of vitamins C and E, and zinc will help prevent varicose veins forming.

USEFUL HERBS: Marigold (p.26), Yarrow (p.20), Hawthorn (p.31), Limeflower (p.62), Bilberry (p.65), Garlic (p.21), Gotu cola (p.27), Plantain (p.52), Rose (p.53)

TREATMENTS:

• To encourage circulation through your veins, take a combination of gotu cola, yarrow, limeflower and hawthorn as teas or standard-dose tinctures, three times a day. Also, eat one clove of raw garlic, or a garlic capsule, every day.

• Relieve any aching or pain by bathing your varicose veins or hemorrhoids with teas of plantain, gotu cola, yarrow or marigold.

• Apply a cold compress of rose water to the area to help to tone the veins and reduce discomfort.

• To strengthen the capillary walls, take a bilberry supplement or standard-dose tincture every day; or add the fruit to your diet.

054 VARICOSE ULCERS

When there is an impeded blood supply to the skin in the legs, often associated with varicose veins (see left), the skin itself can become dry and cracked. If someone or something knocks the affected area, the skin may break and a varicose ulcer may form. If you have poor circulation or a poor diet, are overweight, do not exercise regularly, or sit or stand for long periods of time, you may be susceptible. As well as the remedies below, to reduce swelling, ease soreness and speed up healing of varicose ulcers, place a poultice of honey on the ulcer, then alternate it morning and night with a poultice of comfrey.

USEFUL HERBS: Plantain (p.52), Bilberry (p.65), Gotu cola (p.27), Yarrow (p.20), Garlic (p.21), Hawthorn (p.31), Marigold (p.26), Aloe vera (p.22), Echinacea (p.33), Limeflower (p.62)

TREATMENTS:

- Between dressings, apply teas of healing herbs such as marigold, plantain or gotu cola, or apply aloe vera gel, to the area. Alternatively, dust the area with any of these herbs in powdered form.
- If the ulcer is painful and inflamed, or if it is infected, take ½ tsp echinacea and marigold tincture, three times a day.
- To improve venous circulation take a garlic capsule every day; or take a combination of hawthorn, limeflower, yarrow and gotu cola in a tea, three times a day.

055 VIRAL AND BACTERIAL INFECTIONS

Bacterial and viral infections are involved in most common illness, from colds and flu to chicken pox. When the body is attacked by a foreign microorganism, our white blood cells, and specifically the lymphocytes or B-cells, begin to produce antibodies to fight off the infection. As they rally against the invading microorganisms, we feel unwell – often becoming feverish and generally lethargic. Herbal remedies can be wonderful for not only supporting immune function, but also helping the lymphocytes to do their work, seeing off the infection. At the first sign of infection, drink plenty of fluid to aid the elimination of toxins, and fast to divert energy away from digestion and into the immune system.

USEFUL HERBS: Echinacea (p.33), Licorice (p.39), Garlic (p.21), Lavender (p.42), Sage (p.55), Peppermint (p.46), Elecampane (p.41), Rose (p.53), Milk thistle (p.58), Chamomile (p.44), Rosemary (p.54), Cinnamon (p.29), Ginger (p.69), Coriander (p.30), Lemon balm (p.45)

TREATMENTS:

- Take ¼–½ tsp echinacea, and raw garlic (or a capsule), every two hours during infection.
- Make a tea of either ginger or cinnamon to warm, strengthen and invigorate the digestion. Spices also have antimicrobial properties, making them excellent to ward off infection. Add a little licorice if your infection is viral.
- Drink teas made with aromatic, antimicrobial herbs, such as chamomile, lavender and sage.

THE IMMUNE SYSTEM

056 FEVER

A fever is one of the first outward signs we get that the body's immune system has kicked in to fight an infection, be it viral, bacterial or fungal. A rise in temperature (around 40°C/100°F indicates a moderate fever in adults or children) has a natural antibiotic and antiviral effect on the body, stimulating the infection-fighting white blood cells into action and helping to ward off the infection-causing microorganisms through heat. If we are generally healthy and well-nourished, our body should see off the infection quickly and without difficulty. However, if our bodies are overloaded with toxins – which we can absorb from environmental pollution and from chemicals in our food and drinks; or as a result of a poor elimination of wastes from the bowel, poor sleeping patterns, stress, or little or no exercise – we are likely to suffer from a lack of energy, and lowered immunity and therefore find it harder. It is always better to drink plenty of fluids and to eat little to help the body see off a fever as quickly as possible.

USEFUL HERBS: Basil (p.47), Boneset (p.34), Chamomile (p.44), Cinnamon (p.29), Echinacea (p.33), Cleavers (p.38), Elder (p.56), Ginger (p.69), Lemon balm (p.45), Limeflower (p.62), Meadowsweet (p.36), Peppermint (p.46), Rose (p.53), Rosemary (p.54), Lavender (p.42), Yarrow (p.20), Vervain (p.66)

TREATMENTS:

• To combat the infection take ¼–½ tsp echinacea tincture in a little water, every two hours.

• Make a hot infusion of 2 tsp meadowsweet flowers in 1 cup of boiling water. Take this three to six times a day. Salicin, which is present in meadowsweet, has a similar action to aspirin, lowering fever and easing pain.

• Combine elderflower, yarrow and peppermint in a hot infusion. This is a traditional, but effective, remedy for lowering fever.

• Sponge the body using tepid herbal infusions of elderflower, yarrow, peppermint, lemon balm, limeflower, basil, lavender or vervain, individually or in combination.

• To help reduce fever and overcome infection make a herbal bath using a few drops of the essential oils of lavender, chamomile or basil. Alternatively, use these oils in hand or foot baths or steam inhalations.

• Decoct some ginger root in water for ten to 15 minutes; sweeten the decoction with honey and then drink it as often as you like throughout the day.

• If your child has a fever, try offering chamomile tea. This will not only treat the temperature, but also relax the child sufficiently to ensure a good, restorative sleep. (If your child has a fever that you can't bring down, consult your doctor immediately.)

057 CANDIDIASIS

Candidiasis is a yeast or fungal infection generally caused by the fungus candida albicans. The infection (known as thrush when it occurs in the mouth or vagina) is particularly prevalent in women on the pill, and in those who have recently finished a course of antibiotics, which disturb the balance of microorganisms in the gut. It can also develop when a woman is stressed or run-down. Symptoms include bowel disturbances and an increase in the tendency toward food allergies, with a variety of allergic responses including, eczema, migraines, PMS, cystitis, catarrh, bowel problems, and lethargy.

USEFUL HERBS: Garlic (p.21), Cinnamon (p.29), Burdock (p.24), Fennel (p.37), Marigold (p.26), Rosemary (p.54), Thyme (p.61), Licorice (p.39), Echinacea (p.33), Cinnamon (p.29), Red clover (p.63), Sage (p.55)

TREATMENTS:

- Take teas or capsules of antifungal herbs such as fennel, marigold, rosemary, thyme, cinnamon, red clover and licorice three times a day.
- For thrush in the mouth, chew licorice sticks and make a mouthwash with an infusion of marigold, sage and thyme, and one drop of thyme oil. Use it two or three times a day.
- Dilute ¼–1 tsp of marigold and sage tincture in a little water and use it as a mouthwash, or as a lotion for vaginal thrush.

058 ME/POST-VIRAL SYNDROME

If our immunity is compromised through a diet deficient in essential nutrients, or as a result of stress, recurrent infection, antibiotics or candidiasis, we may not recover in the normal way from an acute viral infection. This then affects other tissues in the body, particularly the muscles and the nervous system. We may have symptoms that persist for weeks or months and, if we are unlucky, even years. These can include muscle aches and pain, depression, weakness, malaise, headaches, insomnia, and restless legs. We can become susceptible to allergies to foods, chemicals and yeast. To increase your energy try supplements of coenzyme Q10, magnesium, B-vitamins and zinc.

USEFUL HERBS: Echinacea (p.33), Licorice (p.39), Wild oats (p.25), Vervain (p.66), Skullcap (p.57), Ginseng (p.49), Garlic (p.21), Cinnamon (p.29), Gotu cola (p.27), Black cohosh (p.28)

TREATMENTS:

- Take standard-dose tinctures of ginseng and gotu cola three times a day – these are adaptogens, which increase resistance to stress.
- Take herbs to alleviate pain and nervous tension, including black cohosh, skullcap, passionflower, vervain and lavender, as teas or standard-dose tinctures three times a day.
- Add to your bath a few drops of the diluted essential oils of thyme, lavender, lemon balm, or rosemary, which help to relieve nervous exhaustion and enhance immunity.

THE IMMUNE SYSTEM

THE IMMUNE SYSTEM

059 ALLERGIES

An allergy or intolerance is the result of an oversensitive immune system, which responds aggressively to substances that generally pose no threat to our well-being (such as pollen, animal dander, house dust mites, or wheat or dairy produce). Asthma, itchy eyes or nose, sneezing, sickness, diarrhea and eczema are all symptoms of the immune system's exaggerated response – an allergic or intolerant reaction. If you suffer from these, a general improvement in your diet can often help to reduce sensitivity – try to cut out caffeine, alcohol and junk food, which can all exacerbate the allergic response. Vitamin C and magnesium act as natural antihistamines, relieving the symptoms of a reaction. Take 500mg of each, twice daily for the vitamin C and daily for the magnesium.

USEFUL HERBS: Echinacea (p.33), Nettle (p.64), Chamomile (p.44), Lemon balm (p.45), Licorice (p.39), Yarrow (p.20), Marsh mallow (p.23), Red clover (p.63), Evening primrose (p.48)

TREATMENTS:

- Drink chamomile and yarrow tea three times a day to soothe the allergic response and inhibit the body's production of histamine, the natural chemical that is responsible for many of the inflammatory symptoms.
- Take teas or standard-dose tinctures of chamomile, echinacea, lemon balm, red clover, wild yam, and yarrow to help your immunity.
- Nettle is a natural antihistamine; try eating nettle soup, or drinking nettle tea.

060 POOR APPETITE

If we feel stressed or unhappy; if we are ill or in shock, dieting or constipated; or if our digestion is poor, we will lose the desire to eat. It stands to reason that if our appetite is poor, our body will not receive all the vital nutrients it needs to function properly, which can lead to myriad health problems. If you suffer from poor appetite, try to eat regularly even if only in small amounts, and try to make what you do eat count by eating healthily. Avoid tea, coffee and alcohol, which suppress the appetite and inhibit nutrient absorption, and try not to drink too much liquid before mealtimes.

USEFUL HERBS: Ginger (p.69), Rosemary (p.54), Fennel (p.37), Dandelion (p.60), Burdock (p.24), Vervain (p.66), Lavender (p.42), Thyme (p.61), Chamomile (p.44)

TREATMENTS:

- Ginger stimulates the appetite and enhances digestion by encouraging the secretion of digestive enzymes. Start the day with a cup of hot ginger tea.
- Take teas of vervain, chamomile, rosemary and thyme to relax the nervous system and to stimulate the flow of digestive juices, and so encourage the appetite.
- Drink teas of dandelion root, chamomile, rosemary and burdock. These are bitter herbs, which again will stimulate the flow of digestive enzymes and promote appetite.

061 OBESITY

With the rise in consumption of unhealthy, processed foods and a decrease in regular physical exercise, obesity is fast becoming a serious problem. In 2004 a study of 30,000 US schoolchildren showed that 15 per cent of 15-year-olds were clinically obese, and more than one third of schoolgirls and almost a third of schoolboys were overweight. The figures were matched by increases in the rates of childhood diabetes, high blood pressure, and sleep apnea (temporary cessation of breathing during sleep), all of which have been linked with obesity. In adults and children alike, obesity can cause all these health problems as well as raised cholesterol, heart disease and strokes, especially if these conditions run in the family. Some people are constitutionally or genetically more prone to weight-gain than others, and low thyroid function and the menopause can lead to a slow-down in metabolism often resulting in weight-gain. But it is safe to say that many cases of obesity are related to overeating, coupled with lack of regular aerobic exercise. Quite simply if the calories we put in are consistently greater than the calories we burn off, we will gain weight. Once our weight-gain is such that our body-mass index (our weight relative to our height; see glossary) is more than 30, we are said to be obese.

When you are trying to lose weight it is important to do so gradually – no more than 1kg (2lbs) a week. Try to cut excess sweet and starchy foods out of your diet altogether as your body will convert any excess into fat immediately. Eat plenty of fresh fruit and vegetables, and meat and fish. Raise your metabolic rate by eating foods that are rich in essential fatty acids, such as oily fish, nuts, seeds and whole grains, and taking supplements of evening primrose and linseed oils. Pineapples and papayas contain enzymes that aid the body's digestion of fats and proteins to aid weight loss. Also, eat walnuts. These are rich in seratonin, the brain chemical that is responsible for the feeling of satiety, and will curb the urge to eat too much. Finally, supplements of chromium, kelp and the resin guggul can help regulate thyroid hormones and raise your metabolic rate.

USEFUL HERBS: Chickweed (p.59), Cleavers (p.38), Fennel (p.37), Garlic (p.21), Black cohosh (p.28), Wild yam (p.32), Linseed (p.43), Plantain (p.52), Ginger (p.69), Cinnamon (p.29)

TREATMENTS:

- Take teas of cleavers, parsley, chickweed and fennel, which have a reputation for aiding weight loss. Certainly they will help to reduce excess fluid in the body, as they are all diuretics.
- If you think that the menopause may have caused your weight-gain, take standard-dose tinctures of wild yam and black cohosh, three times daily, to help to regulate your hormone levels.
- Thirty minutes before a meal, drink 3g psyllium seeds in water. The seeds will help you to feel full and so prevent you from eating too much.
- Add warming spices, such as garlic, cinnamon and ginger, to your diet to stimulate your metabolism.

THE DIGESTIVE SYSTEM

THE DIGESTIVE SYSTEM

062 NAUSEA AND VOMITING

Morning sickness, travel sickness, allergy, food intolerance, migraine, and a bad reaction to medication are just some of the reasons why we might feel and/or be sick. If you experience vomiting without any nausea, peptic ulcer, gastritis, shock, intestinal obstruction, pressure on the brain by a tumour, or problems with balance owing to an ear infection are all potential causes, so consult your doctor immediately. If you are sick remember to keep drinking water, little and often, to prevent dehydration. If your symptoms persist, or if you have vomiting and a high fever, see a doctor.

USEFUL HERBS: Ginger (p.69), Chamomile (p.44), Fennel (p.37), Peppermint (p.46), Thyme (p.61), Echinacea (p.33), Cinnamon (p.29), Garlic (p.21), Bilberry (p.65), Meadowsweet (p.36), Lavender (p.42), Basil (p.47)

TREATMENTS:

- To help settle the stomach, sip ginger tea or beer, or chew small pieces of fresh ginger root; or take regular cups of peppermint or fennel tea.
- If you have food poisoning or a stomach infection, take garlic, ½ tsp echinacea tincture and a cup of chamomile tea, every two hours.
- Take regular cups of cinnamon tea to help settle nausea and combat a stomach infection.
- Eat plenty of bilberries, which will help fight the infection and soothe an inflamed gut.
- If stomach irritation is causing nausea, take regular cups of marsh mallow tea.

063 DIARRHEA

When the bowel becomes overrun with toxins or microorganisms, or if it becomes irritated or inflamed, our stools become loose in an attempt to cleanse the bowel quickly. This is acute diarrhea. Leave it to run its course, but drink lots of water to replace lost fluid, and take electrolyte supplements (available in sachets from your pharmacist). If it persists, especially in children, consult a doctor. More chronic diarrhea may be related to stress, a poor diet or absorption of fats, an infection, bowel disease, or a food allergy or intolerance. See your doctor about chronic diarrhea.

USEFUL HERBS: Cinnamon (p.29), Marsh mallow (p.23), Yarrow (p.20), Meadowsweet (p.36), Peppermint (p.46), Chamomile (p.44), Lemon balm (p.45), Wild yam (p.32), Thyme (p.61), Ginger (p.69), Fennel (p.37), Lavender (p.42), Skullcap (p.57), Basil (p.47)

TREATMENTS:

- Take a tea or standard-dose tincture of yarrow, chamomile or meadowsweet every two hours for acute diarrhea; three times daily for chronic diarrhea.
- Drink ginger and cinnamon tea throughout the day to relieve griping in the bowel and combat infection. For diarrhea with abdominal pain, take yarrow, basil, thyme or peppermint tea.
- For stress-related diarrhea, take teas of chamomile, basil, lemon balm, skullcap, lavender, or wild yam to help relax the gut.

064 CONSTIPATION

Lack of exercise, "holding on" when you need to pass a stool, liver problems, old age, piles, diverticulitis, a food allergy or intolerance, candida, certain drugs (including morphine and codeine), too many refined foods and insufficient fibre in your diet, stress-related bowel tension, and iron supplements can all cause constipation. Never ignore the condition as reabsorption in the bowel forms toxins, which may then cause chronic disease. Taking at least 30 minutes' exercise a day can encourage regular bowel movements. However, if you have an ongoing problem, or if your constipation is sudden or painful, see a doctor.

USEFUL HERBS: Linseed (p.43), Licorice (p.39), Ginger (p.69), Dandelion (p.60), Burdock (p.24), Chamomile (p.44), Lemon balm (p.45), Boneset (p.34), Basil (p.47)

TREATMENTS:

- For a really stimulating laxative, take a mixture of licorice, ginger, dandelion root and burdock tincture (standard dose), three times a day.
- If your constipation is stress-induced, add lavender or lemon balm to your chosen laxative herbs.
- Psyllium seeds and linseeds provide a more gentle laxative. They "bulk out" the stool encouraging it to move along the bowel. Soak 1 or 2 tsp of the seeds in a cup of hot water for two hours, then drink the mixture just before you go to bed.

065 IRRITABLE BOWEL SYNDROME (IBS)

Irritable bowel syndrome is a condition in which an overactive bowel causes a vicious cycle of constipation and diarrhea, often accompanied by wind and griping pain. Studies have shown that one in three cases of IBS result from the sufferer having some kind of food allergy or intolerance and poor digestion, although a poor diet, candida, and particularly stress may also be to blame. If you suspect that you have IBS, take steps to improve your diet and optimize the health of your gut by taking acidophyllus tablets daily. Try to avoid common food allergens, including wheat, dairy produce and gluten. If at any time you experience mucus or blood in your stools, or you have severe griping pains in your abdomen, consult a doctor.

USEFUL HERBS: Wild yam (p.32), Chamomile (p.44), Peppermint (p.46), Yarrow (p.20), Marsh mallow (p.23), Hops (p.40), Bilberry (p.65), Meadowsweet (p.36), Wild oats (p.25)

TREATMENTS:

- To ease the bowel take wild yam and chamomile as a tea or standard-dose tincture, three to six times a day.
- To relieve pain, diarrhea and constipation, and other symptoms linked with IBS, unless you have an intolerance to salicylates, take soothing cups of meadowsweet tea.
- If your IBS is characterized by diarrhea, take bilberry fruit tea. Simmer 2 tbsp dried bilberries in 600ml (1 pint) water for ten minutes. Take ½–1 cup, three times a day.

THE DIGESTIVE SYSTEM

THE DIGESTIVE SYSTEM

066 POOR ABSORPTION

The gut secretes enzymes (which trigger digestion) and the small intestine is lined with tiny villi – finger-like projections that increase the surface area of the gut to maximize the absorption of nutrients from food. Poor secretion of digestive enzymes and damage to the villi as a result of (among other things) inflammation, infection, sudden changes in diet (such as a too high-fibre or low-fat diet), candida, and too many wheat-based foods, can cause poor absorption. In turn this can lead to low energy levels, defects in tooth enamel, diarrhea and fatty stools (that are pale and float), flatulence, distension, weight loss, easy bruising, osteoporosis, and anemia.

USEFUL HERBS: Ginger (p.69), Marsh mallow (p.23), Burdock (p.24), Fennel (p.37), Coriander (p.30), Chamomile (p.44), Rose (p.53), Lemon balm (p.45), Lavender (p.42), Cinnamon (p.29), Thyme (p.61), Elecampane (p.41)

TREATMENTS:
- Start the day with fresh ginger tea (ginger stimulates the digestive enzymes).
- Before and after meals chew coriander or fennel seeds. These can stimulate the flow of digestive enzymes and promote absorption.
- Or, before and after meals, sip teas of digestive herbs, such as chamomile, fennel, rosemary, thyme, ginger, cinnamon or coriander.
- If poor absorption is stress-related, take teas of chamomile, lemon balm, fennel or rose.

067 HEARTBURN AND ACIDITY

When stomach acids travel back up the esophagus (which connects the throat to the stomach) we experience the sharp, burning sensation known as heartburn. Stress, and rich, fatty or spicy foods will all trigger heartburn, as will highly acidic foods such as tomatoes or citrus fruit. Alcohol, chocolate, sugar, refined carbohydrates, tea, coffee, and cigarettes are also common culprits. The condition is aggravated by bending over, sitting hunched up, and lying in bed, as well as by pregnancy, chronic constipation and obesity.

USEFUL HERBS: Ginger (p.69), Aloe vera (p.22), Meadowsweet (p.36), Peppermint (p.46), Chamomile (p.44), Licorice (p.39), Marsh mallow (p.23), Fennel (p.37), Lemon balm (p.45), Dandelion (p.60), Burdock (p.24), Eyebright (p.35)

TREATMENTS:
- Before you eat drink a cup of decocted licorice or dandelion root and burdock. These bitter herbs will help to stimulate proper digestion, helping to prevent the acidic reflux.
- Protect the delicate lining of the esophagus by taking 25ml (1 fl. oz) aloe vera juice twice daily. Aloe vera also aids proper digestion.
- Relax spasm in the gut by massaging essential oils gently into the upper abdomen. Use 2 drops chamomile or lemon balm oil diluted in 1 tsp warm sesame oil.
- If you feel heartburn coming on, chew some fennel seeds to help to ease spasm in your gut.

068 DIVERTICULITIS

Diverticula are small pockets in the bowel wall. When feces gets trapped in these pockets, the diverticula flare up and become infected (diverticulitis), causing griping pain, constipation, diarrhea and wind. The condition is most common in people aged over 50 and is associated with a diet deficient in fibre and too high in refined foods. Lack of exercise and prolonged constipation will also contribute. To prevent diverticulitis, try to eat high-fibre foods, such as whole grains and cooked fruit and vegetables (but not bran, nuts and seeds, and fruits with seeds, which can irritate the bowel). Eating pineapple and papaya are particularly therapeutic as they are rich in certain enzymes that aid digestion and help to prevent diverticulitis. Finally, drink lots of fluid (but avoid caffeine) and take regular exercise.

USEFUL HERBS: Wild yam (p.32), Chamomile (p.44), Ginger (p.69), Licorice (p.39), Marsh mallow (p.23), Peppermint (p.46), Garlic (p.21), Linseed (p.43), Plantain (p.52), Wild oats (p.25), Hops (p.40)

TREATMENTS:
- To soothe and protect the bowel wall from inflammation, three times a day take 25ml (1 fl. oz) aloe vera juice and plantain, or marsh mallow as teas or standard-dose tinctures.
- Drink regular cups of chamomile tea to relieve pain and inflammation in the bowel.
- Eat raw garlic, or take a garlic capsule, twice a day. Garlic helps to fight the bacteria that lodge themselves in the diverticula.

069 FLATULENCE

There is nothing unusual or concerning about a little wind after eating certain foods – beans, cabbages and Brussels sprouts are common culprits, as well as eating lots of raw food or eating too quickly. However, if we are nervous or agitated (which makes us gulp), or if we have a food allergy or intolerance, poor digestion, or are constipated, flatulence can become chronic – which is both embarrassing and painful. Try to eat a healthy diet, and particularly eat pineapple and papaya, which promote proper digestion.

USEFUL HERBS: Wild yam (p.32), Peppermint (p.46), Fennel (p.37), Rosemary (p.54), Chamomile (p.44), Lemon balm (p.45), Basil (p.47), Thyme (p.61), Ginger (p.69), Cinnamon (p.29), Garlic (p.21), Coriander (p.30), Elecampane (p.41), Parsley (p.51)

TREATMENTS:
- Take carminative (flatulence-releasing) herbs, such as basil, rosemary, peppermint, ginger, cinnamon, fennel, lemon balm, and chamomile. Add them to cooking; or take them as teas or tinctures (a few drops in warm water), before or after meals.
- Dilute 2 drops cinnamon, ginger or peppermint essential oil in 1 tsp warm sesame oil and gently massage it into your abdomen to break up and release any wind in your gut.
- If wind is related to an imbalance of bacteria in your gut, eat plenty of garlic and thyme.

THE DIGESTIVE SYSTEM

THE DIGESTIVE SYSTEM

070 GASTRITIS AND PEPTIC ULCERS

Gastritis is the inflammation of the stomach lining, usually caused by irritation of the gut lining and excess acid, which eventually can lead to the formation of peptic ulcers in either the stomach or the small intestine. Poor digestion, poor eating habits, and nervousness or anxiety can all contribute to the condition, which can then be aggravated by smoking; drinking alcohol, tea and coffee; eating fatty foods and pickles; and taking certain medicines. In some cases a bacterial infection (of the Helicobacter pylori bacteria) will cause the condition. If you have a history of ulcers and experience intense pain in your abdomen, you should see a doctor.

USEFUL HERBS: Chamomile (p.44), Licorice (p.39), Marsh mallow (p.23), Plantain (p.52), Meadowsweet (p.36), Marigold (p.26), Aloe vera (p.22), Burdock (p.24), Coriander (p.30), Fennel (p.37), Hops (p.40), Rose (p.53), Yarrow (p.20), Peppermint (p.46)

TREATMENTS:
- Soothe inflammation in the gut by taking teas of plantain, licorice, or marsh mallow three times a day.
- To relieve inflammation, heal ulcers and treat any infection, take strong chamomile tea, or ½ tsp chamomile tincture in a glass of warm water, on an empty stomach four times a day.
- Take 25ml (1 fl. oz) aloe vera juice twice a day to relieve pain and protect the lining of the gut from a profusion of acidity.

071 GALL-BLADDER PROBLEMS

The gall bladder is a small sac that stores bile until the body needs it to break down fats from our food. Gallstones are solid deposits of crystalline substances, such as cholesterol, bile pigments and calcium salts, that can form in the gall bladder. A gallstone that is stuck in the bile duct, which takes bile to the small intestine, causes great pain (and potentially jaundice). If this leads to inflammation or infection in the gall bladder itself, we can find it hard to digest some foods, and experience pain in the gall bladder and stomach. If you have acute pain or develop jaundice, see a doctor.

USEFUL HERBS: Dandelion (p.60), Wild yam (p.32), Lemon balm (p.45), Licorice (p.39), Fennel (p.37), Chamomile (p.44), Yarrow (p.20), Vervain (p.66), Milk thistle (p.58), Rosemary (p.54)

TREATMENTS:
- If you experience acute pain and inflammation take chamomile tea every two hours.
- To relieve pain and inflammation in the gall bladder try a combination of milk thistle, dandelion root, wild yam, lemon balm, vervain and licorice in a tea, three to six times a day.
- For chronic problems take teas of milk thistle, dandelion root, yarrow, wild yam and chamomile three times a day.
- Once the condition has cleared, continue to take wild yam, dandelion root, and chamomile tea three times a day for two to three months to prevent the problem recurring.

072 HALITOSIS

Halitosis – more commonly known as bad breath – may be related to a variety of causes, including bacterial infections in the mouth or throat, a dry mouth, smoking, bad oral hygiene, dieting, diabetes, food lodged in the deep indentations of the tonsils, medications, anxiety, worms, poor digestion, and low excretion of digestive enzymes. Rhinitis (hay fever) and catarrhal congestion can also cause bad breath, as can eating lots of spicy or aromatic foods, such as garlic. However, the vast majority of bad breath originates from accumulated dental plaque (a sticky deposit that coats the teeth and is made up of bacteria, food deposits and degenerated gum), and from food that remains coated on the back of the tongue. The plaque and stale food can then affect the health of the gum tissues and lead to gum disease, which in turn leads to halitosis.

As well as taking herbal remedies to detoxify your system and clear bacteria from your mouth, try the following approaches to avoid and deal with bad breath. Drink at least 2 litres (3½ pints) warm water daily to wash away mucous and bacteria from the mouth and to keep it flowing freely with saliva (which itself helps to clear bacteria). Use a tongue scraper every day to remove the coating on the tongue, and floss your teeth regularly to prevent plaque building up between each tooth. (All these actions not only help to remove the odour problem, but also lower the overall level of bacteria in the mouth and so have a positive effect on the general health in the mouth.) Avoid eating too many heavy, indigestible foods, such as bread, cheese, yogurt, and red meats, as well as too much junk food, which all add to a toxic environment in the digestive tract. Visit your dentist regularly to have your teeth cleaned and to check whether or not you have a bacterial problem with your teeth or gums.

USEFUL HERBS: Aloe vera (p.22), Thyme (p.61), Peppermint (p.46), Rosemary (p.54), Sage (p.55), Dandelion (p.60), Burdock (p.24), Lavender (p.42), Linseed (p.43), Cinnamon (p.29), Ginger (p.69), Parsley (p.51)

TREATMENTS:

• Rinse the mouth with an antiseptic mouth rinse for at least two minutes at a time, every day. Use teas of thyme, sage, rosemary, peppermint or lavender or dilute ½ tsp of their tinctures in a little water. These herbs will also stimulate the flow of saliva if you have a dry mouth.

• Three times daily take ginger, cinnamon, thyme, rosemary, dandelion root and burdock tea, which will enhance digestion and help to eliminate toxins from the body.

• At night use 2 tsp linseeds to clear toxins, either in a smoothie, porridge or a little warm water.

• Try chewing a little parsley after mealtimes to help banish the stale odour of your food. Alternatively, you can chew cardamom seeds which can sweeten your breath and have antiseptic properties as well.

THE DIGESTIVE SYSTEM

073 WORMS

Threadworms, which are white, threadlike and up to 13mm (½ inch) long, are the most common type of intestinal worms, and especially common in children. They are caught easily by simple acts such as sharing books and pens, and touching doorknobs. Apart from causing itching and soreness around the anus, worms can cause stomach pain, halitosis, and bowel upsets, as well as sleep-disruption and teeth-grinding. The female worm moves from the bowel to the anus at nighttime to lay her eggs. If you think that your child may have worms, inspect his or her anus just before bed – you may be able to see one or two worms. All children should wash their hands after playing outside, and before mealtimes. Anyone with worms should avoid heavy dairy foods, such as cheese and ice cream, which create a habitable environment for worms; and eat lots of pineapple and papaya, warming spices (such as ginger and cinnamon), and ground pumpkin seeds, all of which help to expel worms.

USEFUL HERBS: Thyme (p.61), Lavender (p.42), Garlic (p.21), Basil (p.47), Aloe vera (p.22), Gotu cola (p.27), Elecampane (p.41), Ginger (p.69)

TREATMENTS:
- To prevent egg-laying and to soothe irritation, mix 2 drops basil, lavender or thyme oil in 1 tsp sesame oil; apply it to the anus before bed.
- Chop finely 1 or 2 cloves of garlic and mix them with either 1 tbsp honey, or some carrot juice, or a little warm milk and drink it half an hour before breakfast every day.

074 MOUTH ULCERS

Even though mouth ulcers tend to be tiny, they can cause a great deal of pain. Cuts caused by sharp teeth, badly fitting dentures, the immune system's attack on the lining of the mouth, or inflammation in the digestive tract can all cause mouth ulcers. Overall, they are usually an indicator that the body is run-down as a result of, say, stress, illness or drugs, or that it is deficient in B12, folic acid, or iron. All these things cause a shift in the ecological balance in the mouth, which in turn can lead to a mouth ulcer. As a first line of defence, build up your general health by eating nutritiously and taking time to relax and reduce stress.

USEFUL HERBS: Bilberry (p.65), Sage (p.55), Marsh mallow (p.23), Lemon balm (p.45), Thyme (p.61), Lavender (p.42), Chamomile (p.44), Plantain (p.52), Ginger (p.69), Peppermint (p.46), Aloe vera (p.22)

TREATMENTS:
- Ease the pain and speed the healing of ulcers using daily mouthwashes of marsh mallow, lavender, chamomile and/or plantain.
- To overcome infection and cool inflammation, use antiseptic mouthwashes of sage, echinacea, thyme, lemon balm or bilberry three times daily.
- Relieve pain using local anesthetics, such as mouthwashes, or sprays of ginger, chamomile, peppermint and lemon balm tea.
- Protect the ulcer and prevent it worsening by applying aloe vera gel.

075 FLUID RETENTION

Retaining excess water (edema) tends to make us feel uncomfortable, puffy and heavy, particularly around the abdomen and in the feet. Fluid retention is common in pre-menstrual women, as well as during pregnancy and the menopause. Poor circulation and varicose veins are also causes, and the condition can be related to chronic deficiencies in protein, vitamins and minerals, and a diet that is high in salt. Chronic edema can be related to serious problems, including kidney and heart conditions.

USEFUL HERBS: Dandelion (p.60), Cleavers (p.38), Plantain (p.52), Chamomile (p.44), Meadowsweet (p.36), Fennel (p.37), Rosemary (p.54), Nettle (p.64), Burdock (p.24), Yarrow (p.20), Vitex (p.67), Wild yam (p.32), Parsley (p.51), Chickweed (p.59), Vervain (p.66)

TREATMENTS:

- To clear excess water from the body, drink teas of diuretic herbs – yarrow, meadowsweet, fennel, cleavers, nettle, plantain, burdock and chamomile – at least three times a day.
- For fluid retention associated with PMS or the menopause, add hormone-balancing herbs, such as vitex and wild yam, to your diuretics. Dandelion leaves and cleavers are good for tender, swollen breasts.
- Add to bath water 2 drops essential oils with diuretic actions diluted in 1 tsp sesame oil. Try fennel, rosemary or chamomile.

076 KIDNEY STONES

Kidney stones are concentrated lumps of substances such as calcium oxalate, calcium phosphate, magnesium ammonium phosphate, cystine, and uric acid. When a kidney stone moves it causes sudden, terrible pain. This in turn can cause sweating, nausea and vomiting. Eventually, most stones make their way naturally into the bladder and the pain is gone – although this process can take anywhere between a few minutes and several days. To help prevent kidney stones, make sure that your diet gives you plenty of phosphates (found in milk, nuts, pulses and oats) and protein, and that it is low in oxalates (found in coffee, black tea, rhubarb, sorrel and spinach). Finally, drink lots of fluids (2–3½ litres/4–6 pints of water a day).

USEFUL HERBS: Marsh mallow (p.23), Fennel (p.37), Bilberry (p.65), Parsley (p.51), Passionflower (p.50), Dandelion (p.60), Chamomile (p.44), Lemon balm (p.45), Nettle (p.64), Cleavers (p.38), Meadowsweet (p.36)

TREATMENTS:

- To help prevent and treat kidney stones, drink two or three cups of nettle and parsley tea daily.
- Take a combination of dandelion leaves, cleavers, bilberry and marsh mallow in a tea, to help dissolve and wash out stones and "gravel".
- Add to the above tea antispasmodic herbs, such as chamomile, fennel and lemon balm, to lessen the spasm in the ureters, and passionflower to ease the pain.

THE URINARY SYSTEM

077 CYSTITIS

Cystitis is an acute urinary infection that tends to affect women rather than men (women have a shorter urethra, making it easier for bacteria to travel into the urinary tract). The infection causes a frequent urge to urinate, pain on urination and the feeling that you cannot fully empty your bladder. You might also have abdominal pain and fever. To prevent cystitis drink 3–4 litres (5–7 pints) of fluid a day, and avoid tea, coffee and alcohol which irritate the urinary system. If an infection hits drink 1 tsp baking powder in water twice a day to neutralize the urine's acidity and relieve pain.

USEFUL HERBS: Chamomile (p.44), Fennel (p.37), Lemon balm (p.45), Marsh mallow (p.23), Yarrow (p.20), Bilberry (p.65), Nettle (p.64), Garlic (p.21), Burdock (p.24), Gotu cola (p.27), Coriander (p.30), Wild yam (p.32), Meadowsweet (p.36), Plantain (p.52), Dandelion (p.60), Vervain (p.66)

TREATMENTS:

- Take teas of soothing herbs such as marsh mallow and plantain to relieve the pain and ease the irritation in the urinary tract.
- Eat bilberries, or take them as a juice or powder, to prevent a build-up of bacteria in the urinary tract and to flush out existing bacteria.
- Fight the infection by taking lukewarm yarrow, chamomile, lemon balm or fennel tea, individually or in combination. Drink the tea every two hours for an acute infection and three times a day for a chronic problem.

078 PROSTATE PROBLEMS

The prostate is a male gland that wraps around the urethra, the tube that carries urine from the bladder to the penis. Although prostatic enlargement can occur as a result of infection or cancer, it is usually related to falling levels of testosterone (particularly in men in their mid- to late-40s), and the conversion of testosterone into dihydrotestosterone (DHT, which partly is responsible for sperm maturation). An enlarged prostate obstructs the flow of urine, causing urinary hesitancy followed by an urgency to pass water. However, the swollen gland also prevents the bladder from emptying properly, which means that sufferers become prone to urinary infections, and will often have disturbed sleep as a result of nighttime trips to the toilet. If you suffer from prostatic enlargement, eat a high-protein diet to encourage good testosterone-production, and eat lots of cooked tomatoes, which are rich in lycopene, an antioxidant that helps to maintain prostate health. Eat half a cup of pumpkin seeds every day. Their high zinc content hampers the work of certain enzymes that cause an enlarged prostate. Always refer prostate problems to your doctor.

USEFUL HERBS: Echinacea (p.33), Vitex (p.67), Nettle (p.64), Licorice (p.39), Plantain (p.52)

TREATMENTS:

- Licorice prevents the conversion of testosterone to DHT. Take ½ tsp licorice tincture in 100ml (3½ fl. oz) water, once a day.
- If your prostate is inflamed or infected, take teas of nettle root or echinacea three to six times a day.

079 BREAST BENIGN DISORDER

Benign mammary dysplasia (BMD; also known as fibrocystic breast disease) causes the breasts in some women to feel lumpy and tender, particularly during the week before their period. The condition is related to an imbalance in estrogen levels. It is aggravated by caffeine and other substances, known collectively as methlyxanthines, in coffee, tea, chocolate and cola, but potentially helped by the gammalinoleic acid (GLA) in evening primrose oil, and by supplements of vitamin E. Problems in the breasts are usually benign, but always investigate a breast problem quickly with a doctor.

USEFUL HERBS: Evening primrose (p.48), Vitex (p.67), Wild yam (p.32), Burdock (p.24), Milk thistle (p.58), Marigold (p.26), Black cohosh (p.28), Dandelion (p.60), Cleavers (p.38), Lavender (p.42), Red clover (p.63)

TREATMENTS:
- Balance your estrogen levels by taking teas or standard-dose tinctures of vitex or wild yam daily. If your breasts are particularly painful, add black cohosh and dandelion root. Add burdock, milk thistle and/or marigold to aid the detoxifying work of the liver.
- Aid lymphatic drainage and clear congestion in the breasts by drinking marigold or cleavers tea, three times a day.
- Massage your breasts gently every day, using 2 drops relaxing lavender essential oil in 1 tsp warm sesame oil.

080 PRE-MENSTRUAL SYNDROME (PMS)

Pre-menstrual syndrome, a hormonal imbalance that affects some women in the run-up to their period, involves physical, mental and emotional changes ranging from mood swings, headaches and insomnia to diarrhea, constipation and acne. As well as herbal remedies, try supplements of evening primrose oil, and calcium, magnesium and the vitamins E and B-complex, which can all significantly relieve symptoms of PMS.

USEFUL HERBS: Evening primrose (p.48), Vitex (p.67), Meadowsweet (p.36), Chamomile (p.44), Cleavers (p.38), Burdock (p.24), Dandelion (p.60), Wild yam (p.32), Lemon balm (p.45), Rosemary (p.54), Skullcap (p.57), Vervain (p.66), Peppermint (p.46), Milk thistle (p.58), Black cohosh (p.28), Fennel (p.37)

TREATMENTS:
- To balance your hormone levels take ½ tsp vitex tincture half an hour before breakfast.
- Take teas or standard tinctures of burdock, milk thistle, dandelion root, or rosemary three times a day to help the liver to break down hormones.
- To relieve fluid retention and bloating, take teas of diuretic herbs, such as meadowsweet, chamomile, cleavers, burdock, or dandelion leaf, three to six times daily.
- To ease headaches take teas or standard-dose tinctures of chamomile, rosemary, vervain and/or peppermint.

THE REPRODUCTIVE SYSTEM

081 PAINFUL PERIODS (DYSMENORRHEA)

There are many causes of painful periods, including emotional problems, poor circulation, muscular tension, smoking, lack of exercise, stress, tiredness, caffeine, bad posture, shallow breathing, hormone imbalances, and a deficiency in essential fatty acids, magnesium, vitamins B6 or C, zinc or iron. The condition causes anything from a deep, dragging sensation in the lower abdomen to severe cramping.

USEFUL HERBS: Wild yam (p.32), Black cohosh (p.28), Chamomile (p.44), Lemon balm (p.45), Rosemary (p.54), Thyme (p.61), Rose (p.53), Ginger (p.69), Cinnamon (p.29), Licorice (p.39), Yarrow (p.20), Marigold (p.26), Lavender (p.42), Vitex (p.67), Skullcap (p.57), Coriander (p.30), Meadowsweet (p.36), Sage (p.55), Limeflower (p.62), Vervain (p.66),

TREATMENTS:

- Wild yam, chamomile, lemon balm, rosemary, thyme and rose will all relax spasm and tension in the uterus. Take them as teas or standard-dose tinctures, three to six times a day.
- If you have intense cramps with scanty bleeding take hot ginger or cinnamon tea to improve circulation to the uterus, and ¼–½ tsp black cohosh tincture, with 5 drops licorice tincture, to ease the pain, three times a day.
- Give yourself a gentle abdominal massage using 2 drops lavender or rosemary essential oil diluted in 1 tsp sesame oil.

082 HEAVY PERIODS (MENORRHAGIA)

Heavy periods may be caused by a hormonal imbalance, stress, low-thyroid function, uterine fibroids, endometriosis, or nutritional deficiency, particularly of iron, protein, essential fatty acids, calcium, magnesium, and vitamins C and E. Women using an IUD (inter-uterine device) or approaching the menopause also commonly suffer heavy periods. Without treatment heavy periods can lead to anemia.

USEFUL HERBS: Black cohosh (p.28), Yarrow (p.20), Limeflower (p.62), Bilberry (p.65), Hawthorn (p.31), Wild yam (p.32), Vitex (p.67), Rose (p.53), Dandelion (p.60), Milk thistle (p.58), Marigold (p.26), Cinnamon (p.29), Nettle (p.64), Plantain (p.52)

TREATMENTS:

- Help to reduce bleeding by taking black cohosh, rose and yarrow either as teas or standard-dose tinctures, individually or combined, three to six times daily.
- Strengthen your blood vessels by taking yarrow, limeflower, bilberry or hawthorn tincture (standard dosage), three times a day.
- If your heavy periods are cause by polyps, endometriosis or fibroids, take a combination of vitex, wild yam, black cohosh and rose as a tea or 1 tsp tincture, three times a day.
- Regulate your hormones with ½ tsp vitex tincture taken 30 minutes before breakfast.

083 IRREGULAR PERIODS

If a woman has an irregular menstrual cycle, she has a hormonal imbalance. Some of the most common causes are stress, overwork, trauma, and exhaustion as a result of illness. Other triggers include low thyroid function, menopausal changes, drugs, allergy or intolerance, dietary deficiencies (particularly of iodine, manganese, chorine, essential fatty acids, zinc, calcium, iron and magnesium, and vitamins B6, C and E), being overweight or underweight, and excess travel.

USEFUL HERBS: Vitex (p.67), Wild yam (p.32), Red clover (p.63), Hops (p.40), Licorice (p.39), Burdock (p.24), Milk thistle (p.58), Dandelion (p.60), Ashwagandha (p.68), Gotu cola (p.27), Wild oats (p.25), Vervain (p.66), Skullcap (p.57), Lemon balm (p.45), Sage (p.55), Ginger (p.69)

TREATMENTS:

- To help normalize your hormone levels take wild yam, red clover, hops and/or licorice tincture (standard dosages), three to six times daily.
- Vitex in particular will help to regulate the hormones by its action on the pituitary gland. Take ½ tsp of the tincture half an hour before breakfast, every day.
- Take burdock, milk thistle or dandelion root, in teas or standard-dose tinctures, to help the liver to break down excess hormones.
- If the root of the problem is stress, take teas of ashwagandha, gotu cola, wild oats, skullcap or vervain to support the nervous system.

084 FIBROIDS

Fibroids are benign, non-painful growths of smooth muscle tissue on the wall of the uterus. If the growths are large they tend to cause heavy menstruation, as well as a frequent need to pass urine, incontinence, an enlarged abdomen, constipation, and anemia (as a result of excess blood loss). Estrogen makes fibroids grow, and low levels of estrogen can shrink them, so many sufferers find that after the menopause their fibroids become smaller and almost disappear. If you are overweight with excess estrogen in your system, you will probably be more prone to fibroids, so try to eat healthily and take plenty of regular exercise.

USEFUL HERBS: Vitex (p.67), Wild yam (p.32), Yarrow (p.20), Rose (p.53), Thyme (p.61), Ginger (p.69), Lemon balm (p.45), Chamomile (p.44), Burdock (p.24), Dandelion (p.60), Milk thistle (p.58), Marigold (p.26)

TREATMENTS:

- Take hormone-regulators, such as vitex and wild yam, as standard-dose tinctures three times a day. To clear toxins from the pelvis, combine these with yarrow, rose, thyme and/or ginger.
- Take herbs, such as wild yam, lemon balm, thyme, chamomile and rose as teas or standard-dose tinctures, three times a day, to help relax the uterus and reduce pain and congestion.
- Take teas or standard-dose tinctures of liver herbs, such as burdock, dandelion root and milk thistle, to help to break down excess estrogen.

THE REPRODUCTIVE SYSTEM

THE REPRODUCTIVE SYSTEM

085 OVARIAN CYSTS

There are many types of ovarian cysts, but the most common are those that occur as a result of incomplete ovulation. They are generally related to hormonal imbalances and possibly to low thyroid function. If the cysts are small they cause no symptoms; but if they are large they can cause abdominal swelling, pain during intercourse, pressure on the bladder, irregular periods or no periods at all, and infertility. If a woman has many cysts, she may have polycystic ovarian syndrome, which may be caused by an excess of the male androgen hormones in her system. Supplements of B-vitamins and vitamin E, and a healthy diet with plenty of fresh fruit and vegetables, whole grains, nuts and seeds will help to keep hormones in balance.

USEFUL HERBS: Vitex (p.67), Wild yam (p.32), Black cohosh (p.28), Milk thistle (p.58), Dandelion (p.60), Burdock (p.24), Ginger (p.69), Rose (p.53), Rosemary (p.54), Marigold (p.26)

TREATMENTS:

- To balance hormones take ½ tsp vitex tincture each morning half an hour before breakfast.
- Take reproductive tonics wild yam and black cohosh as standard-dose tinctures.
- Milk thistle, burdock and dandelion root will help the liver to break down excess hormones. Take them as teas or standard-dose tinctures.
- Massage your lower abdomen each day before a shower or bath, with 2 drops ginger, rosemary or rose oil in 1 tsp sesame oil.

086 ENDOMETRIOSIS

Endometriosis occurs when endometrial tissue, which normally lines the inside of the uterus, grows in other sites in the pelvic region, such as on the ovaries and in the fallopian tubes. The growth of this tissue through the course of the menstrual cycle causes pelvic congestion, which means that obstructions and fibrous adhesions may form between the uterus and the bowel. These adhesions can hamper fertility and conception. Symptoms of endometriosis include sharp, stabbing often intense abdominal pains that are aggravated by sex; back pain that worsens before a period; and pain associated with bowel movements.

USEFUL HERBS: Ginger (p.69), Licorice (p.39), Marigold (p.26), Vitex (p.67), Black cohosh (p.28), Rose (p.53), Wild yam (p.32), Yarrow (p.20), Chamomile (p.44), Vervain (p.66), Lavender (p.42)

TREATMENTS:

- Take ½ tsp vitex tincture half an hour before breakfast each morning to help to balance your hormones.
- Take teas or standard-dose tinctures of black cohosh, licorice or wild yam, three to six times a day, to help to maintain your hormonal balance and to relieve uterine inflammation.
- If you suffer intense pain, take teas or standard-dose tinctures of pelvic relaxants, including chamomile, vervain, rose or lavender, combined with ginger (to enhance pelvic circulation), every hour or two if necessary.

087 VAGINAL INFECTIONS

Most vaginal infections are yeast infections, known as thrush (which are caused by the candida albicans fungi), although trichomonas vaginalis and gardenerella vaginalis can also cause infection. The microorganisms proliferate when the natural pH balance of the vagina is disturbed through such things as hormonal imbalances, antibiotics, stress, poor diet, the pill, pregnancy, post-menopausal changes, and diabetes. Vaginal infections are often associated with lowered estrogen levels during the menopause, as the pH of the vagina is estrogen-dependent.

USEFUL HERBS: **Marigold (p.26), Garlic (p.21), Thyme (p.61), Sage (p.55), Cinnamon (p.29), Lavender (p.42), Chamomile (p.44), Echinacea (p.33), Rosemary (p.54), Coriander (p.30)**

TREATMENTS:

- Take antimicrobial herbs – echinacea, marigold, thyme, cinnamon or sage three to six times a day against infection.
- Peel a clove of garlic without nicking it. Wrap the clove in clean gauze and attach a clean, unbleached string to create a tampon. Repeat each night for six consecutive nights.
- Add 1 tsp fresh garlic juice to 2 or 3 tbsp yogurt, and use it as a douche twice daily.
- Add a few drops of chamomile or lavender oil to douches, creams, lotions and tampons.
- Sit in a bowl of chamomile tea for 15 to 20 minutes to soothe the infection and soreness.

088 MENOPAUSAL PROBLEMS

For most women the menopause begins at around age 50. It may be preceded by the perimenopause, when periods may become more or less frequent, and menopausal symptoms may come and go. During the menopause the levels of a woman's reproductive hormones – estrogen and progesterone – decline until menstruation ceases. In the West we tend to think of the menopause as a period of identity crisis for women, but many cultures celebrate this new era in a woman's life. Hot flushes, loss of libido, palpitations, a dry vagina and mood changes can all be symptoms of this hormonal change. Try to avoid alcohol, caffeine, and hot spices, which can exacerbate the symptoms; and take daily supplements of vitamin E and evening primrose oil to help ease them.

USEFUL HERBS: **Black cohosh (p.28), Wild yam (p.32), Sage (p.55), Marigold (p.26), Fennel (p.37), Hops (p.40), Chamomile (p.44), Evening primrose (p.48), Elder (p.56), Red clover (p.63), Nettle (p.64), Vitex (p.67), Ashwagandha (p.68), Rose (p.53)**

TREATMENTS:

- Take ½ tsp ashwagandha tincture in warm milk morning and night for several months during the perimenopause.
- Ease menopausal symptoms by taking hormone-balancers. Take teas or standard-dose tinctures of black cohosh, wild yam, vitex, hops, red clover or marigold three times a day.
- Add rose, chamomile or sage to your chosen tea (above), specifically to relieve hot flushes.

THE REPRODUCTIVE SYSTEM

THE REPRODUCTIVE SYSTEM

089 LOW SEX DRIVE AND IMPOTENCE

A decrease in sexual interest, and in men an inability to maintain an erection, are often the side-effects of an illness such as diabetes, drugs such as antidepressants, or stress or exhaustion. Circulatory problems, raised cholesterol, and high blood pressure can all contribute to problems with sex drive, as can the falling hormone levels that come with increasing age. Psychological issues, such as marital problems, guilt, depression, anxiety, and lack of confidence are all culprits, too. Try to avoid a diet that includes too many sugary foods (although chocolate can improve your sex drive) and refined carbohydrates, and lower your intake of alcohol. If you smoke try to give up.

USEFUL HERBS: Ashwagandha (p.68), Cinnamon (p.29), Vitex (p.67), Wild oats (p.25), Ginseng (p.49), Parsley (p.51), Rose (p.53), Wild yam (p.32), Basil (p.47), Ginger (p.69), Rosemary (p.54)

TREATMENTS:

- For low libido in women, take teas or standard-dose tinctures of rose, wild yam, ashwagandha or vitex, singly or combined, three times a day.
- For low libido in men, take 1 tsp ashwagandha powder in warm milk morning and night.
- To reduce stress and increase libido in both men and women, eat plenty of wild oats, and take one 500mg capsule of ginseng a day.
- Enjoy sensual massage with stimulating essential oils: 2 drops either basil, ginger, cinnamon or rosemary oil in 1 tsp sesame oil.

090 LOW SPERM COUNT

It takes around 100 days for sperm to develop. During this time the sperm are susceptible to damage from a number of sources, including overheated testes as a result of over-hot baths, undescended testes, and tight underpants. In addition infections such as mumps, as well as high fevers, stress, diabetes, hormone imbalances, poor diet, caffeine, smoking, alcohol, drugs, and being overweight or underweight can all affect sperm production. Cut out junk foods, caffeine, alcohol and nicotine, and try to eat healthily and take regular exercise. Estrogens in the food chain can upset the balance of male hormones. Choose organic meat (hormones are added to some animals to bulk them out), and avoid drinking tapwater, because water-purification cannot remove the hormones that we excrete. Ideally avoid any plastic-wrapped food or drink, especially if it has been left in the sunlight (heat causes the plastic to break down and leak its chemical constituents into the contents of the container). Take supplements of kelp, B-vitamins, vitamin E, zinc, essential fatty acids, and coenzyme Q10.

USEFUL HERBS: Ashwagandha (p.68), Wild oats (p.25), Licorice (p.39), Ginger (p.69), Garlic (p.21), Ginseng (p.49)

TREATMENTS:

- Take tonics for the reproductive system – wild oats, ashwagandha, licorice or ginger – as teas or standard-dose tinctures, three times a day.
- To balance your hormones and increase your resilience to physical and psychological stress, take capsules of garlic and of ginseng regularly.

091 MINOR BURNS AND SCALDS

Friction, chemicals, and excess heat can all burn the skin. Most burns result from accidents at home. If the scald or burn is small, affects only the superficial layer of skin (the burned patch may swell and appear red), and you act promptly with some simple herbal first aid, you can relieve the pain and speed the skin's healing with minimum or no scarring. Before applying anything to the burn, immerse the area in cold water for five to ten minutes, or until the pain subsides. Raise the affected area slightly to slow blood-flow there, and to ease the pain. If the burn forms blisters, do not burst them in case they later become infected. Cover the burn with a loose, dry dressing. Consult your doctor if the herbal remedies below do not reduce the pain, or if a burn does become infected or more painful.

USEFUL HERBS: Lavender (p.42), Aloe vera (p.22), Chamomile (p.44), Elder (p.56), Plantain (p.52), Rose (p.53), Echinacea (p.33), Marigold (p.26), Yarrow (p.20), Marsh mallow (p.23), Cleavers (p.38), Evening primrose (p.48), Chickweed (p.59), Limeflower (p.62), Linseed (p.43)

TREATMENTS:

• Apply aloe vera juice or neat lavender oil repeatedly until the pain begins to subside.

• Apply a compress of chamomile, elderflower, plantain, or rose water to the burn. Repeat frequently to relieve pain and speed healing.

• If the dressing becomes stuck to the skin, soak it off with a warm decoction of an antiseptic herb, such as echinacea or marigold.

092 MINOR CUTS AND WOUNDS

As soon as you puncture or graze your skin, hold the wound under cold running water until it is thoroughly clean. If the cut is deep, bring the two sides together and bind them with surgical tape. Then, visit your doctor as gaping cuts carry a risk of tetanus. Use herbal remedies to clean the wound before binding it (thus protecting it from infection), and to constrict the blood vessels to stem bleeding.

USEFUL HERBS: Yarrow (p.20), Peppermint (p.46), Lavender (p.42), Plantain (p.52), Marigold (p.26), Aloe vera (p.22), Gotu cola (p.27), Cinnamon (p.29), Elecampane (p.41), Basil (p.47), Chickweed (p.59), Nettle (p.64)

TREATMENTS:

• Yarrow has excellent astringent properties, making it great to stem bleeding. Apply yarrow tincture directly to a gauze and place it over the wound; or bathe the wound in yarrow tea.

• If you can find fresh plantain, take a few leaves and crush or chew them and then apply them moist to the wound to stop the bleeding. If you have no fresh plantain, use a little tincture.

• If the wound is very painful, bathe it regularly with peppermint or lavender tincture diluted in a little warm water.

• Place 4 or 5 drops marigold tincture in a little warm water and wash the wound. Marigold has antiseptic properties.

FIRST AID

093 SPLINTERS

Always remove splinters quickly. Although most splinters are simply a little irritating, if they are left untreated, they can turn septic and lead to infection. First rub a little antiseptic remedy into the area and, if the splinter is easy to hold on to, pull it out using tweezers. However, if the splinter is buried under the skin, apply a hot poultice or soak the affected area in hot water or a herbal tea for ten to 15 minutes. Repeat several times over the course of a day. Once the splinter surfaces you can pull it out. You may need to use a sterilized needle to ease it through. If the splinter is large or involves glass, seek medical advice.

USEFUL HERBS: Marigold (p.26), Chamomile (p.44), Plantain (p.52), Thyme (p.61), Marsh mallow (p.23), Garlic (p.21), Lavender (p.42), Aloe vera (p.22)

TREATMENTS:

• Soak the splinter in a strong antiseptic tea of marigold, chamomile, plantain or thyme.

• To draw the splinter to the surface make a marsh mallow compress and apply it to the affected area as often as possible. After each application rub in some marigold or chamomile cream.

• If the area is red and swollen, soak it in marigold tea. Or, crush some garlic, wrap it in a piece of gauze, and bandage it over the area.

• To prevent infection in the wound, apply a few drops of neat lavender oil.

094 BRUISES

A bruise occurs when the blood vessels beneath the skin burst, but the skin itself does not rupture. If you bruise easily, you may be deficient in vitamin C and bioflavonoids (both found in citrus fruit). Bruises without an obvious cause can be an early sign of anemia or a deficiency in vitamin K, or of leukemia or other cancers, so you need to tell your doctor. Note that an extensive bruise may indicate that you have a serious underlying injury, such as a broken bone or damaged internal organ. If the pain in such a bruise worsens over 24 hours, consult your doctor.

USEFUL HERBS: Ginger (p.69), Bilberry (p.65), Chamomile (p.44), Lavender (p.42), Rosemary (p.54), Burdock (p.24), Evening primrose (p.48), Chickweed (p.59), Yarrow (p.20), Linseed (p.43), Parsley (p.51)

TREATMENTS:

• Crush some fresh parsley and apply it to the bruise repeatedly, as often as possible. The bruise should clear in a day or two. Alternatively, you could apply yarrow tea to the bruise as a lotion.

• Speed healing and calm inflammation by gently massaging the bruised area with 2 drops chamomile, lavender or rosemary essential oil in a base of 1 tsp sesame oil.

• Take bilberry every day. Bilberry is rich in vitamin C and bioflavonoids and over time will help to strengthen the capillary walls.

095 SPRAINS AND STRAINS

A sprain occurs to a muscle and its tendon; a strain, to a ligament. Both types of injury will cause pain, swelling, bruising and stiffening. Sprains and strains are generally a result of overuse or over-stretching, which in turn are often because of a fall or sports accident. When you injure yourself, immobilize the area, apply a cold compress or ice packs to help reduce the pain and swelling, and then support the sprain or strain with an elastic bandage. Try to elevate the injury above heart-level, which helps to drain blood and fluids from the muscle or joint, and reduces swelling. Apply a poultice, and bandage the area firmly. Change the dressing twice daily. Certain dietary tactics will help to reduce inflammation. Add turmeric to your diet to reduce swelling, or take ½ tsp in a little hot water, twice a day. Eat lots of pineapple, which contains the anti-inflammatory enzyme bromelain. If your pain worsens 24 hours after the injury, consult a doctor.

USEFUL HERBS: **Marigold (p.26), Yarrow (p.20), Aloe vera (p.22), Ginger (p.69), Linseed (p.43)**

TREATMENTS:

- To reduce pain and inflammation apply a compress made using a tea of marigold or yarrow; or freeze these infusions into ice cubes. Once they are ready, wrap the ice cubes in cotton or gauze and apply them to the area.
- Again to reduce pain and inflammation, massage the area using equal amounts of ginger juice and sesame oil; or two parts aloe vera gel and one part yarrow tincture.

096 NOSEBLEEDS

Nosebleeds tend to occur more frequently in children and the elderly as the tiny blood vessels in the lining of their noses are very fragile. In adults a blow to the nose, an infection, or a dried-out nose as a result of central heating can all cause nosebleeds. Frequent nosebleeds may be a sign of high blood pressure or a blood-clotting disorder. When you have a nosebleed, hold your nostrils together firmly and lie down with your head back until the bleeding stops. Do not blow your nose or sniff, which could dislodge the clot and start the bleeding again.

Eat plenty of vitamin C and bioflavonoids (found in citrus fruit) to strengthen the capillary walls and to help prevent frequent attacks. Sometimes you can stop a nosebleed just by drinking cold water. Or, traditional wisdom suggests that sniffing a mixture of cider vinegar and a little water will stop the bleeding. A few drops of cypress oil inhaled from a handkerchief may also do the trick. Note: if after a blow to the head you experience frequent nosebleeds, you may have a fracture. Seek immediate medical help.

USEFUL HERBS: **Rose (p.53), Marigold (p.26), Yarrow (p.20), Cinnamon (p.29), Nettle (p.64)**

TREATMENTS:

- Apply a cold compress of rose water, or of 1 or 2 tsp marigold or yarrow tincture diluted in a little cold water to the back of the neck to stem bleeding.
- Hold cotton wool soaked in rose water or in yarrow tincture to the nose and inhale.

FIRST AID

097 INSECT BITES AND STINGS

The immune system's response to an insect's saliva or venom causes pain, itching, swelling and redness, and in severe reactions, swelling in our airways.

To prevent being bitten cover your skin as much as possible, especially at dawn and dusk, when insects such as mosquitoes are most likely to bite. Apply lavender oil liberally to the skin and eat plenty of garlic. Make your own repellent oil by placing 5 drops citronella, lavender, tea tree or rosemary oil in 1 tsp sesame oil, and apply it to the skin. Place an oil burner in your room and in it drop rosemary, sage or eucalyptus oil to keep the insects at bay.

If you are stung by a bee remove the sting by pressing it out sideways with your thumbnail, rather than pulling it. Press or suck out any poison. For a wasp sting, if there is nothing else to hand, a little urine can be an excellent first-aid remedy. Try not to scratch mosquito bites as this may introduce infection.

USEFUL HERBS: Lavender (p.42), Garlic (p.21), Rose (p.53), Sage (p.55), Rosemary (p.54), Cinnamon (p.29), Plantain (p.52), Marsh mallow (p.23)

TREATMENTS:

- For bee stings apply either lavender oil, crushed garlic, rose water, or a sage tea.
- For wasp stings apply rose water, cinnamon or lavender oil, or crushed plantain leaves.
- For ant bites rub in raw garlic.
- For mosquito bites apply lavender or rosemary oil, or garlic or rose water.

098 TRAVEL SICKNESS

Travel sickness is the result of a mix-up in the messages that the brain receives from the eyes and ears during motion. Normally the eyes gather visual data that tell the brain, via the inner ear, where the body is and in which direction it is going. Certain things, such as reading in the car, can confuse the nervous system about the data it is receiving from the eyes, resulting in travel sickness. The condition can make you feel sleepy, dizzy, cold and clammy, breathless, sweaty, and nauseous. If you feel sick try to look out of a window and, if you can, let in some fresh air. If you are on a boat, remain on deck and look at the horizon to help get your balance mechanisms working properly. To try to prevent travel sickness altogether, get lots of sleep before you travel and avoid heavy, fatty meals and alcohol. Drink plenty of fluids throughout the journey to prevent dehydration.

USEFUL HERBS: Ginger (p.69), Peppermint (p.46), Meadowsweet (p.36), Fennel (p.37), Chamomile (p.44), Cinnamon (p.29), Wild yam (p.32), Basil (p.47)

TREATMENTS:

- Chew on a little fresh ginger root to settle your stomach, or take a flask of ginger tea and sip it when you need to.
- Inhale some calming and balancing essential oils: basil, rosemary and peppermint are all excellent for travel sickness.
- Suck on a peppermint to ease nausea and keep digestive energy going in the right direction.

099 SUNBURN

The sun's powerful, ultraviolet rays can cause premature wrinkling in the skin and, more seriously, are associated with skin cancer. It goes without saying that prevention is far better than any remedy, and we should all keep our skin covered and out of direct sunlight as much as possible. Fair-skinned people are particularly at risk as their skin produces only small amounts of melanin (dark skin pigment) on exposure to the sun, making them burn more easily. If you are out in the sun, cover up, and drink plenty of water because the sun is extremely dehydrating. And if you do become sunburned, first soothe the area by bathing it with cool water, or by taking a bath in tepid water. Then apply the following soothing herbal remedies as frequently as you need to. Cover the affected areas when you go outside, even when you are in the shade.

USEFUL HERBS: Aloe vera (p.22), Chamomile (p.44), Marigold (p.26), Nettle (p.64), Chickweed (p.59), Peppermint (p.46), Rose (p.53), Lavender (p.42), Coriander (p.30)

TREATMENTS:

• Apply aloe vera juice, chamomile cream, or marigold ointment to the sunburn.
• Bathe the area with a cool tea of nettle, chickweed, peppermint, chamomile or marigold, or with soothing rose water.
• Add a few drops lavender oil to a cool bath.
• Cool your entire system by drinking teas of rose, peppermint, coriander leaf, or lavender, and by drinking aloe vera juice.

100 TOOTHACHE

Toothache is usually a sign that a particular tooth has a damaged or dying nerve, which is causing infection and swelling. Always see your dentist for toothache as the infection in your tooth can find its way into the bloodstream and infect other parts of your body. If you are unable to see your dentist straight away, follow a few simple rules. Don't eat anything hard as this can exacerbate the pain. Don't eat anything very cold or very hot, as your teeth will be extremely sensitive. Finally, use herbal remedies to relieve the pain.

USEFUL HERBS: Cinnamon (p.29), Chamomile (p.44), Hops (p.40), Passionflower (p.50), Skullcap (p.57), Ginger (p.69), Marigold (p.26), Thyme (p.61), Rosemary (p.54), Rose (p.53), Garlic (p.21), Echinacea (p.33)

TREATMENTS:

• To relieve the pain of toothache, put a little of the essential oils of cinnamon and chamomile on a cotton bud and apply the soaked bud to the area. Or, drink tea of hops, chamomile, passionflower or skullcap three to six times a day. Or, chew fresh ginger.
• Make an antiseptic mouthwash of marigold, chamomile, thyme, rosemary or rose.
• Bruise a clove of garlic (a powerful antibacterial) and hold it next to the infected tooth.
• Drink teas of echinacea, marigold, chamomile, thyme or rosemary, which all have antibacterial properties, three to six times daily.

FIRST AID

Glossary

Italic type denotes words that appear as entries elsewhere in this glossary.

Acute condition/illness: an illness that is intense, but finite and self-contained. Left untreated, some acute illnesses may become *chronic*.

Adaptogen: increases resilience to physical and mental stress, and helps the body to maintain its natural state of equilibrium.

Adrenocorticotrophic: acts to regulate the function of the cortex (the outer layer) of the adrenal glands, which secrete hormones.

Aerial parts: the parts of the plant that grow above the ground, such as the flowers and leaves.

Alterative: aids the eliminative functions of the body, such as sweating, urinating and passing stools, to clear toxins.

Analgesic: relieves pain.

Anthelmintic: eliminates worms.

Anticonvulsant: prevents or relieves convulsions, such as in epilepsy or febrile convulsions.

Antihemorrhagic: stops bleeding.

Antihistamine: prevents the production of *histamine* by tissue cells known as mast cells.

Antimicrobial: destroys disease-causing microorganisms.

Antioxidant: a compound that inhibits and controls the negative effects of *free radicals*. Antioxidants are found in many fresh fruit and vegetables, especially those containing vitamins A, C and E, and the minerals zinc and selenium.

Antispasmodic: prevents or relieves spasms.

Antitussive: relieves coughing.

Anxiolytic: reduces anxiety.

Aperient: mildly laxative.

Astringent: contracts or dries the body's tissues.

Bile: a fluid that is formed in the liver and stored in the gall-bladder, and that aids digestion.

Bitter tonic: a herb with a bitter taste that improves health through its action on the liver.

Body Mass Index (BMI): the figure denoting weight relative to height, developed as a statistical device during the 19th century. To calculate your BMI, divide your weight in kilograms by the square of your height in metres. A healthy BMI figure lies between 20 and 25 (lower than 20 is said to be underweight; higher than 25, overweight).

Carminative: relieves flatulence and spasm in the gut.

Chronic condition/illness: an illness that is ongoing, lasting several months or even years.

Cholagogue: encourages the secretion of *bile* from the gall bladder.

Demulcent: soothes the mucous membranes.

Depurative: removes toxins from the system.

Diaphoretic: brings blood to the skin and stimulates sweating, helping to reduce fevers.

Digestive: enhances the action of the digestive system.

Diuretic: increases the flow of urine.

Emmenagogue: brings on menstruation.

Emollient: softens and soothes the skin.

Expectorant: aids the production of mucus from the chest.

Febrifuge: reduces fevers.

Fibroid: a benign mass of body tissue (tumour), most often occurring in the wall of the womb.

Free radical: an uncharged molecule produced in the body as a result of oxidation. Free radicals can cause damage to otherwise stable cells and are associated with age-related illness, and cancer. They are stabilized by *antioxidants*.

Galactagogue: increases the production of breast milk.

GI tract: gastrointestinal tract – that is, the tract of the stomach and intestines.

Homeostasis: The body's natural state of equilibrium, and the optimum state of well-being.

Histamine: an organic compound released by cells known as mast cells during an allergic reaction; the trigger for the symptoms we know as the body's response to an allergy.

Hypoglycemic: lowers blood sugar.

Hypotensive: lowers blood pressure.

Laxative: increases bowel movements.

Lesion: any wound, ulcer, tumour, and so on, that represents damage to the body's tissues or organs.

Mucilage: a thick, sticky liquid found in many plants that has a soothing action on the human body.

Nervine: has a restorative effect on the nervous system.

Peripheral vasodilator: stimulates the flow of blood to the periphery of the body – that is, the skin, hands and feet.

Probiotic: helps to re-establish the normal bacterial population of the gut, which can be upset by antibiotics or fungal infections.

Refrigerant: reduces body temperature.

Rhizome: an underground stem that grows outward (horizontally) rather than downward.

Rubefacient: produces mild irritation on the skin and thereby increases circulation to the affected area.

Runner: a plant's shoot that typically grows along the surface of the ground.

Salicylate: a plant compound characterized by its bitter, painkilling and antifungal properties. Salicylates are used in the production of aspirin.

Stomachic: enhances the function of the stomach.

Strobile: a cone from a pine, fir or other conifer.

Styptic: curbs bleeding from cuts on the skin.

Thymoleptic: lifts mood.

Vulnerary: heals wounds on the skin.

Index

Picture acknowledgments

The publisher would like to thank the following photographic libraries for permission to reproduce their material. Every care has been taken to trace copyright holders. However, if we have omitted anyone we apologize and will, if informed, make corrections to any future edition.

Page 34 Fotosearch, Waukesha, *35* John Feltwell/ Garden Matters, Kent, *49* Rick Mariani/Photolibrary.com, London, *50* Steven Wooster/ Garden Picture Library, London, *65* Laurie Campbell/NHPA, Sussex

Author's acknowledgments

The author would like to thank Tessa Heron for all her help during the writing of this book.

Publisher's acknowledgments

The publisher would like to thank Beatriz Linhares for her help with the photography, and Peter Jarrett, at the Middlesex University Medical Garden, for his help with finding herbs.